MW00534520

10 THINGS
Everyone
NEEDS TO
KNOW ABOUT
MONEY

LINDA DAVIES

illustrated by
NICK BASHALL

First published in 2021 by Atebol Cyfyngedig, Adeiladau'r Fagwyr, Llanfihangel Genau'r Glyn, Aberystwyth, Ceredigion SY24 5AQ

www.atebol.com

@10thingsmoney

Text copyright © Linda Davies 2021
Illustrations copyright © Nick Bashall 2021

The right of Linda Davies to be identified as the author and Nick Bashall to be identified as the illustrator of this work has been asserted.

All rights reserved.

No part of this publication may be reproduced, stored in a retrieval system, or transmitted, in any form or by any means (electronic, mechanical, photocopying, recording or otherwise), without the prior written permission of the publisher.

Cover design by Tom Burns Creative
Designed by Owain Hammonds

ISBN 978-1-913245-26-9

The author and publisher have made every effort to ensure that the external websites and information contained in this book are accurate and up to date at the time of going to press. The author and publisher are not responsible for the content, quality or ongoing accessibility of the websites.

The publisher acknowledges the financial support of the Books Council of Wales.

Important Note

The information contained or referred to within this book does not constitute any form of advice, representation or arrangement by Atebol Cyfyngedig or the author. As a reader you take full responsibility for making (or refraining from making) any specific investment or other financial decisions. Given that the impact of any information expressed in this book can vary widely depending on your particular circumstances, you should always carry out your own research into any financial products that are of interest to you, including taking appropriate professional advice.

Although the contents of this book are provided in good faith, we do not warrant the completeness, truth or accuracy of the information or other content in this book, or its usefulness for any particular purpose. By reading this book you acknowledge and agree that (i) your use of the information contained within this book is at your own risk and (ii) you bear full responsibility for your own financial research and decisions, and that the author shall not be liable for any action that you or others take, or fail to take, based on your use of, or reliance on, the information contained within or referred to in this book.

This book is dedicated to my late father,
Professor Glyn Davies.

Linda Davies

This book is dedicated to my twin sister,
Suzanne.

Nick Bashall

Contents

Introduction

Money is a language all of its own. It doesn't sit quietly in our pockets or in our bank accounts. Money talks. Sometimes it whispers. Sometimes it roars. It informs how long you live, where and how. What kind of education you receive. What you can do in your free time. *If* you have free time. It influences continents, governments, political systems, economies, war, peace, terrorism, crime and the planet itself. We ignore it at our peril. Sometimes money doesn't want to be heard or seen. Those who control it like encrypting it, either with code or with jargon.

In this book I strip away the jargon and give voice to ten things that will help us better understand and speak the language of money. This fluency will help us to conserve and grow our money, to invest wisely, to avoid the pitfalls that part us from our money, to use but not be enslaved by debt, in short to master money so that it does not master us. In so doing, we will improve much more than just our financial health. We can learn to wield money for the greater good.

If money is power, so too is knowledge.

This is a very personal book for me. My late father, Glyn Davies, was Emeritus Professor of Economics at Cardiff University and his last and greatest book was entitled *A History of Money*. It contained a lifetime's learning, wit and wisdom and won him many prizes and plaudits. It has inspired this book. His own interest in the subject was sparked when he was a boy growing up in the valleys of south Wales. Roaming the hills one day he discovered a hoard of silver Roman coins. And he wondered, who had owned them? And why had they been buried in a wooded valley? What was their story? Those coins had a hidden history and by touching them he was connected with it. (Incidentally, he gave the coins to one of his teachers in search of answers he sadly never found. Nor did he find out what happened to the coins ...)

I was a canny little girl, growing up in the 1970s when UK inflation peaked at 25 per cent and interest rates at 17 per cent. I liked to save and I loved getting my interest statement from the bank showing how *much* my money was growing. While I sat there doing nothing! I found it incomprehensible and fascinating.

When I was five and one of my brothers twelve, we were taking the ferry home from a holiday in Ireland. Both my parents were confined to their cabin by food poisoning so they thrust some money at us and told us to go and buy some food for ourselves. Instead we found the slot machines. I fed them pennies and, lo and behold, I won the jackpot. But my brother was greedy. He managed to convince me that if I kept gambling I would win another jackpot. Despite my instinctive feeling that this was unlikely, I listened to him until I had gambled away almost every penny. We had just enough for one plate of chips, which we shared looking pathetic in the canteen. We went back to our parents and I told them there was a money machine which gave you money. Trouble was it ate all my money so could I please have some more ...

An early lesson in the power of money, the perils of gambling and the risk of addiction.

Still fascinated by money, I studied it at university, reading Politics, Philosophy and Economics at St Edmund Hall, Oxford. I learned about the theory and then about the practice. For the next eight years I worked as an investment banker, a cog in the heart of the money machine in London, New York and Eastern Europe. And then I escaped to write novels about money. In many ways, money was the central character in those books.

I still work in the financial services sector as a Director of an FCA (Financial Conduct Authority) approved and regulated company and as a consultant and adviser to various financial companies.

In this book, I share with you my insider's knowledge.

It's worth £50 because I say it is.
– The Bank of England

Chapter One

What is money?

The biggest confidence trick of all time

Our twenty-first century notes, coins and debit cards are a kind of ethereal, intangible, largely invisible[1] *fiat* money. In Latin, the word *fiat* means 'let it be so'. They are only worth something because we believe they are worth something, because our governments have declaimed 'let it be so', legitimizing them by taking them in payment of taxes, and by decreeing that people must accept them for all debts. For good measure, our governments often further legitimise our fiat money by invoking the divine in the iconography on our notes and coins. 'In God we trust', declare US dollar bills.

Governments effectively wave the magic wand of belief to render otherwise worthless pieces of paper and metal valuable in what is akin to the biggest confidence trick of all time. Think of this as financial abracadabra.

Without the magic spell of belief, as we shall see below, fiat money is worthless.

If we travelled back in time, say to the eighteenth century, armed with one of our twenty-pound notes and a debit card and we attempted to buy a loaf of bread and a pail of milk, we'd likely be thrown in the stocks and pelted with potatoes. The note and the card would be useless because they would have no context: neither king, government nor citizens would recognise them. No one would believe in them and this lack of belief would render them worthless.

Let's contrast this with the forerunner of fiat money: *commodity money* – money that has a use independent of the ability to spend it. Money that has not been 'magicked' into being.

If we conducted our time travel armed with a few gold coins, we would be received with glad cries and open arms because gold is a recognised, useful and coveted commodity. Everyone in eighteenth-century Britain would know all about gold, they would all believe that it could be used to buy goods and services as well as to make valuable jewellery. Other kinds of commodity money used by our ancestors globally were similarly multipurpose – whales' teeth had ceremonial value; cowrie shells, like gold, were originally used as jewellery (and as the illustration on page 6 reveals, could serve a variety of purposes); saucepans speak for themselves, as do iron rakes and arrowheads.

But both fiat and commodity money share a central characteristic. If we don't believe in them, if we can't find a use for them, they become worthless.

We can see this with fiat money in Germany's Weimar Republic (1918–33), an era of hyperinflation, where notes had more value as firewood than as currency and people literally burned them to heat their homes.

And we can see this with commodity money in nineteenth-century Fiji.

In the middle of the century, a trading ship was captured off one of the Fijian islands. On board was a treasure chest, brimful of gold coins. The finders of the treasure found a novel use for them. They played ducks and drakes, skipping the coins of gold across the glittering water. One of the young Fijians who had played with the plundered gold later became a government official after Fiji became a British Crown colony in 1874. Even then, he was still reluctant to accept payment in sterling silver or gold sovereigns. They just didn't mean much to him. He preferred to be paid in the traditional whales' teeth. *Tabua* were sacred and valued far more than 'modern' money.

These examples show that for something to be accepted as money, we need to believe in it. We need to think it has value, that it is somehow *proper*. That's why today, while some people value bitcoin and would happily be paid in it, others wouldn't touch it with a bargepole.

Money is a slippery thing, far more psychological than we might at first think.

Money is only money if we believe it is

How do governments and other authorities pull off this confidence trick? How do they convince people that a seemingly useless piece of paper with words and images is worth anything?

The answer lies in the historical activities of private banks and, before them, goldsmiths.

Back in the 1600s, during the English Civil War (1642–51), individuals and families who wished to keep their gold and jewels safe would deposit them with goldsmiths, who were able to protect them in their fortified vaults. The goldsmiths would sign a piece of paper as a receipt for the valuables, pledging to return them to the owners on production of the piece of paper. This receipt became transferable, enabling the holder to buy goods and services to the values shown. It became paper money, empowered by faith and trust, but underpinned by tangible assets – jewels and gold.

In later centuries, government-owned or government-sponsored central banks got in on the act and decided that issuing paper notes backed up by gold to the face value of the piece of paper was a useful way of transacting business and more sophisticated than the tally sticks[2] used by previous English governments.

This was known as the gold standard. The UK, the US and many other countries backed up their currencies with gold. In theory, anyone possessing a note, say a ten-dollar or ten-pound note, could go to the central bank and exchange that note for a sliver of gold worth the same amount.

However, as global economies grew, there was insufficient gold to exchange.

The Great Depression, which began in the US in 1929, spread to the UK and across the world, causing investors to lose confidence in the British pound. They did not believe there was sufficient gold in the UK's vaults to exchange for banknotes. The ensuing panic created a self-fulfilling prophecy as everyone dashed to swap their notes for gold before it ran out. Faced with the annihilation of their gold reserves, the Bank of England abandoned the gold standard in 1931.

The US held out until 1971, finally giving up the gold standard during the financial exigencies of the Vietnam War, because it operated as a brake on their ability to borrow and spend.

Fiat money and the divorce from gold

Today, the pound, the dollar and currencies around the globe cannot be exchanged for precious metals or commodities and have value only by fiat, only because we believe they do. And, in a wonderful, virtuous circle, believing makes it so.

But why do we believe the government?

Because they have power. They possess the printing press. They can literally print money.[3] They control the armed forces and the police, they raise taxes – crucially, they accept the fiat currency as payment of those taxes – they employ many of us, they spend the national currency on our behalf. All that legitimises the currency and gives us faith that it is useable and valuable today, useable and valuable tomorrow, and will continue to be so next year – in short, that it is a safe haven for our savings.

Banknotes issued in the United Kingdom make a promise to us: 'I promise to pay the bearer on demand the sum of £20'. Of course, it would be nonsensical to take a twenty-pound note into the Bank of England and receive another twenty-pound note in exchange, but the value here is not practical, it is conceptual. What it is really saying is 'believe in the value of this note because the mighty Bank of England (and hence the government of the United Kingdom) believes in it'.

So, my dad's in cowrie futures.

The state uses a varying iconography of power to reinforce the strength of this promise and of our belief.

In Britain we have an image of the Queen on our notes. In the US, a revolving deck of former presidents adds legitimacy. US notes are emblazoned with a promise of their own: 'This note is legal tender for all debts, public and private'. The reverse shows the image of the White House surmounted by the pledge 'In God we trust'. British coins similarly invoke divine power. They have the letters 'FD' engraved upon them, an abbreviation of the Latin *Fidei Defensor* or 'Defender of the Faith', a title given to the reigning English monarch since Henry VIII. It was in the eighteenth century that 'Fid Def' or 'FD' began to be emblazoned on British coins. It was left off the new two-shilling piece in 1849, which became known subsequently as the 'godless florin'. Deeply unpopular, it was quickly redesigned.

God and Mammon do mix

They always have. If we cast our mind back thousands of years to the pre-Christian temples of Mesopotamia we see gods and Mammon living in happy harmony.

Temple loans, in which gods appear as creditors, have been discovered in a study made by Rivkah Harris of the archive of the wonderfully named Sin Temple in Tutub (present-day Khafajah in Iraq). Harris's research reveals the prominent role played by the temple as a kind of bank, lending silver and food.

The British Museum holds a clay tablet dating from 1823 BC which was excavated at Sippar in southern Iraq. Inscribed upon it is the following: 'Puzurum son of Ili-Kadri has received 38 1/6 shekels of silver from the god Shamash, he will pay interest at the rate set by Shamash, at the time of the harvest he will repay the silver and the interest on it.'[4]

The priest made the loans. With a god as a creditor, borrowers tended to repay.

Another example showing that money is built on trust occurred during the siege of Valletta by the Turks in 1565. The Ottomans imposed an embargo on Valletta and supplies of everything ran short, including gold and silver. The ruling Knights of Malta were forced to use copper to make the coins they needed to pay their people. Stamped upon the coins was the legend *Non aes sed fides* ('Not money, but trust').

So money is and always has been legitimised by power. By trust. By belief. It is no coincidence that the word *credit* comes from the Latin *credere*, 'to believe'.

But what happens when that power and belief and trust falter?

We saw this recently in Venezuela, where people stopped trusting the government and its fiat currency.

Responsible governments run their economies in a prudent way, raise money through taxes, borrow money to bridge the gap between their own income and expenditure, and stay within acceptable limits of borrowing. Irresponsible governments borrow excessively and, when no one will lend them any more money, they simply print their own to pay for things they could not otherwise fund. This is what the government of Venezuela has done. This artificial expansion of the money supply causes a rise in prices as more money chases the same number of goods. (The International

Monetary Fund estimated in 2018 that Venezuela's inflation rate was 929,797 per cent.)

This inflation effectively reduces the purchasing power of the notes and coins in circulation. The public begins to lose confidence that they are worth their face value. Typically, they try to rid themselves of that currency before its value falls even more and are reluctant to accept that currency in payment for goods and services they sell. They look for alternatives. Like the US dollar. Or barter. Or bitcoin (it's no surprise that Venezuela has been one of the earliest and biggest adopters of bitcoin, mining it ferociously).

Venezuelans stopped believing in their fiat currency, the bolívar. As a result, the fiat currency collapses and dies and is replaced with another.

When one token representing money dies, another form springs to life, of necessity.

In short

Money is only money if we believe it is. Belief, and currencies, can and do die. If you live in a country where you suspect that belief in the fiat currency is faltering, or will begin to falter, try to amass, if possible, foreign currencies that you can trust: the US dollar, which is viewed as the 'reserve currency' of the world, or the UK's pound sterling, typically viewed as one of the next safest currencies in the world. Gold coins are another good option.

Chapter Two

Where does money come from?

The strange magic of new money

How is money born? How does it come into circulation? You might think that the creation of money is the province of the government. Indeed, in the UK the government is responsible for printing banknotes (the De La Rue company prints the actual notes) and, via the Royal Mint, minting coins. But, as we have seen, these are a tiny fraction of our overall money (3 per cent in 2017). A whopping 79 per cent of our NEW money is created privately by banks such as HSBC, Lloyds, Barclays, Santander and so on.[1] To see how they create this money we need to look at their business model, which goes roughly as follows:

1 Savers deposit their money in either current accounts to which they can get access at any time, or savings accounts where they generally have to give say a month's or six months' notice to withdraw the cash.
2 In return (and generally only on savings accounts) the banks pay interest. If the rate of inflation is low, as it is now, the banks pay only a low rate of interest. As the rate of inflation rises so, generally, does the nominal[2] rate of interest.

So far, so non controversial. But it's what the bank does next that gets controversial, and reproductive. It lends your deposit out to other people. Some find that hard to fathom.

One of my favourite anecdotes tells how, in the 1950s, a notoriously distrustful potentate was visited by the representative of a British bank. As we show in the illustration opposite, the banker tried to convince him that rather than hiding his money under one of his palace's many mattresses he might be better off putting it in a bank.

'So, what will you do with it then?' he asked. 'Will you keep it safely locked away?'

'We shall make it work for you,' answered the rep. 'We will lend it out to other people.'

'What?' exploded the potentate. 'You will take MY money and GIVE it to complete strangers???'

The potentate had a point. This, in essence, is what commercial banks do. They don't give it away, obviously; they lend it. But they don't just lend what you deposit with them. They lend out multiples of that. And, in the lending out, a strange magic is unleashed. New money is conjured from thin air.

How much new money is born depends on, primarily, the size of the bank's fractional reserve, that is, the percentage of the deposit the bank keeps on hand so it can cough up cash should a depositor want some snappish.

Fractional reserve banking – making money elastic

The process here is essentially making money stretch. A lot. And taking precautions so that if the money elastic snaps no one gets stung. You could also regard it as putting money to work.

In the US, the reserve requirement on current accounts at large banks is 10 per cent. The UK, Canada and Australia have no reserve requirement.[3] These countries rely instead mainly on capital requirements the banks need to lodge with the central bank to prevent them from loaning/creating new money with too much wild abandon. But let's say the actual reserve is 10 per cent. So, if a deposit of £1,000 is made, the bank keeps £100 on hand to satisfy depositor withdrawals and can make loans of £900. It does this simply by crediting the borrower's bank account. Meanwhile, the original depositor still has a balance in their account that shows £1,000. With a few strokes of a keyboard, new money has been created by a bank manager sitting in an office. From thin air.

The new money, the fresh £900, is now being spent, maybe on some DIY, on a TV, on a kayak, on a rare book, on a pedigree hamster ... circulating round the wheel of the economy. Working hard. Quite a bit of it ends up as new deposits in other banks (or the same one again). Those deposits then form the springboard for more loans. Let's assume for argument's sake that £800 of the £1,000 ends up being deposited in bank accounts. The banks will then keep £80 as a reserve and then lend out a fresh new loan or loans of £720. Of brand spanking new electronic money. Which will be spent and circulated through the economy, much of it ending up deposited back in banks again. And so it goes on in a wonderful cascade of new money creation. Data suggests that a whopping total of over £9,000 of new money would be created in this way. A sum of £1,000 has been stretched to nine times its length.

And the most interesting thing is, this new money has been created not by the central bank but by commercial banks – that is, by the private sector.[4] It seems amazing that something so important and potentially dangerous resides in private hands. But it does. The government can influence how much money is created by the private sector by raising interest rates and making borrowing less attractive, and by raising the level of the fractional reserve banks are required to lodge. But this is tinkering round the edges.

Quantitative easing – dangerous medicine

That's not to say that central banks don't get involved in creating new money. They do, and how! The central banks' response to the global financial crisis (primarily the US Federal Reserve, the Bank of England, the European Central Bank and the Bank of Japan) was to create staggering amounts of liquidity/new money via quantitative easing or QE, a kind of alchemy where they turn debt[5] into new money which then lubricates the financial system. Essentially, central banks create new money out of thin air (with a few strokes of a keyboard) and use this to buy 'financial assets' from private banks. These assets are mostly bonds, debts issued by the government itself and also by private sector companies. The money paid to the banks for these bonds can then be loaned out in the same way as other deposits to (hopefully) stimulate the economy, or can be held as part of the reserves of that bank.

By the end of 2017, the US Federal Reserve had spent $4.5 trillion, the Bank of England £435 billion, the European Central Bank €2.5 trillion and the Japanese Central Bank ¥443.6 trillion (source: the central banks).

Injecting liquidity into a system teetering on the brink of collapse was essential and detractors have failed to come up with a better way of dealing with the crisis and preventing an even bigger one. But, as always, there was a cost. The new money did what new money so often does. It did not create new things, it just raised the prices of existing things – in this case financial assets like shares and bonds, and real assets, like property – making the rich richer and those without assets relatively poorer and less able to haul themselves onto the property ladder.[6] It also involved interest rates falling to historically low levels, effectively impoverishing many savers, conservative people who might have had reason to think they were insulating themselves against financial shocks by keeping their savings in cash. QE was like administering a powerful opioid to ease the pain. Trouble was, governments got addicted and carried on using long after they should have stopped. Many of the side effects have already been felt. Others are looming, yet to manifest.

In short

Governments produce money via the printing press. They also create money by alchemical operations in the financial markets, with dangerous side effects. But the overwhelming majority of new money is created by the private sector through bank loans.

Chapter Three

What is the future of money?
Rebels and revolution

Is cash dead?

Commentators often predict that we are heading for a cashless society. Electronic money in our bank accounts is super convenient. It cannot be stolen in the way that cash bulging from your wallet or pockets can be (although debit and credit cards are stolen or cloned every second of the day).

Banks are also keen to encourage the use of electronic payments at the expense of cash. Bank of America spends a whopping $5 billion each year processing cash and cheques and servicing cash machines (nearly 10 per cent of its cost base).[1] Equally, governments and law enforcement agencies dislike cash as it can be used for nefarious criminal or terrorist activities and to evade taxes.

According to UK Finance, the growing convenience of electronic money and the ease of contactless payments have seen the proportion of cash used in all payments in the UK fall from 62 per cent in 2006 to 40 per cent in 2016 and further still to 28 per cent in 2018. They predict that by 2028 cash use will have fallen to 9 per cent. Those predictions were made before the coronavirus pandemic hit, further accelerating the trend away from cash. In the UK, in the week leading up to March 2020, the use of cash fell by 50 per cent as consumers switched to online shopping and to electronic, contactless payment methods to avoid the risk of handling contaminated notes and coins.

In Sweden, considered to be the most cashless society in the world, only 19 per cent of payments by volume are made using cash (as of 2018). The government loves this – VAT receipts are up 30 per cent over five years as a result.[2] Cash accounts for only 2 per cent of the total value of transactions in the country and this was expected to fall to less than half a per cent by 2020.[3] That was before taking into consideration the effect of coronavirus.

In a move which might have seen our ancestors burnt at the stake for witchcraft four hundred years ago, more than 4,000 Swedes have had microchips implanted in their hands, enabling them to pay for rail and bus travel, food and public toilets, and to enter keyless offices, with a wand-like wave of their hands.

Cash would appear to be facing an existential threat. John Howells, the chief executive of Link, the UK's largest free-to-use ATM operator, has warned that it will struggle to maintain its network without government intervention. Between 2018 and 2020, 9,500 free ATMs were taken out of circulation (17 per cent of the total UK network) and 1,200 bank branches have closed. How can we use cash if we cannot get our hands on it?

Should we worry about the decline of cash? Yes! There are considerable downsides to electronic money and many upsides to cash.

Cash dependence

For millions of elderly customers and other vulnerable groups, cash is a necessity. They do not use or understand non-cash forms of banking and payments. Natalie Ceeney, chairwoman of the Access to Cash Review, says: 'Our research showed that for around eight million adults (17 per cent of the UK adult population) cash is an economic necessity. And, contrary to widespread perception, it's not age which is the biggest indicator of cash dependence but poverty.'[4]

Any move to do away with cash would be catastrophic for these people.

Liberty

Dostoevsky called money 'coined liberty'.[5] Cash offers freedom and anonymity whereas electronic money can be traced. Everyone knows what you're up to: Google, Amazon, the government, fraudsters.

Practicality

Cash is more robust. Phone batteries can go flat. Electronic money can disappear. Periodically, and for various reasons, banks' IT systems crash. In April 2018, half of TSB's online banking customers were unable to access their accounts for over a week. The wonderfully named Paul Pester (who has now bailed out as chief executive on a golden parachute) said the bank was 'on its knees'.[6] It has since recovered but faces fines and compensation claims amounting to £60 million.

Bank accounts can be hacked by criminals or by states engaged in cyber warfare. Entire payment systems could be shut down. How then would our economies function without cash? How would people buy food or medicines?

For all these reasons, a significant proportion of individuals, most of them NOT criminals, are very resistant to the idea of doing away with cash entirely.

Beauty and history

Banknotes have a power and a beauty that can never be replicated by squiggles on a flickering screen.

Electronic money is wonderful in the same way that emails are wonderful but we still love letters. Letters say things and have an import that an email never can. We keep precious letters and cards written to us; they become part of our history.

Banknotes tell a story. I was given the selection opposite by a friend who called them the *Tyrant Collection*. Who is in power at a given time and who fell to make way for them? Whom do we wish to memorialise? What mantras do we value sufficiently to inscribe upon our notes? What terrible ravages has hyperinflation inflicted on a currency, as seen in the absurdly high denomination banknotes of inflation-plagued countries? Banknotes and coins answer all these questions and more. They give historians precious information. For the rest of us, they form part of the historical backdrop to our lives, which we would miss if they were to disappear.

China: Mao Tse-tung

Iran: Ayatollah Khomeini

Uganda: Idi Amin

Iraq: Saddam Hussein

Turkmenistan: Niazov

North Korea: Kim Il Sung

King Cash

In fact, in defiance of the predictions of many economists, futurists and those at the cutting edge of innovation such as Elon Musk of Tesla (who has opined that cash will soon disappear), we are amassing more cash, not less, than in the past. Torsten Slok, chief economist of Deutsche Bank, reveals that the number of 100-dollar bills in circulation globally has doubled since 2008 to 12.5 billion. Another report[7] shows that, as of 2018, cash in circulation relative to GDP (gross domestic product – a measure of the size of the economy) has increased to 9.6 per cent across all continents, up from 8.1 per cent in 2011. The Bank of England reports that in 2016 roughly £70 billion of cash circulated in the UK, twice as much as a decade earlier. This is NOT explained by inflation, which has been low over that period.[8] I suspect it *is* explained by growing distrust of the financial system following the 2008–09 global financial crisis, by fears about IT meltdowns and hacking, and by the fact that with historically low – even negative rates of interest – stuffing it under the mattress rather than paying the bank to sit on it looks ever more attractive and logical. Cash is not going out without a fight.

Rebellious money

In that unlikely hotbed of unrest, Sweden, a rebellion is underway. The former head of INTERPOL heads a campaign group called Cash Rebellion, or *Kontantupproret*, in support of cash. He fears technical glitches and cyber warfare. A cashless Sweden could be unprepared if faced with a crisis.

All the factors above suggest that, in part, and for some people, cash will always be king.

There is also an important psychological component to cash besides the security it offers us: it acts as a brake on our spending.

The money illusion

Does what we use as money affect our financial behaviour? The answer to this question is yes: when we pay for goods with electronic money we are more likely to overspend. The graph below shows household debt as a percentage of net disposable income and its relationship to non-cash transactions as a percentage of all transactions.

Debt dangers: The move to a cashless society might imply higher levels of consumer credit

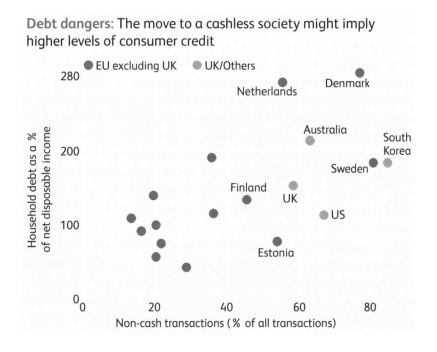

The data reveals that the less we use cash as a percentage of our overall expenditure, the more we borrow. Electronic payments would appear to make us more likely to overspend, possibly because

there is a sense of illusion, unreality and deferred consequence when we spend electronic money. When we dig notes from our wallet, the sense of spending and the awareness of a diminishing supply of notes are immediate and real.

Electronic money tempts us to overspend, which in turn can be damaging to our mental health. As Mr. Micawber notes in Charles Dickens's novel *David Copperfield*: 'Annual income twenty pounds, annual expenditure nineteen nineteen and six, result happiness. Annual income twenty pounds, annual expenditure twenty pounds ought and six, result misery.'

Seemingly attractive but potentially dangerous 'buy now pay later' schemes perpetuate the money illusion and are becoming ever more popular.

The Money and Mental Health Policy Institute, set up by financial guru Martin Lewis, notes[9] that shoppers are more likely to sign up to such schemes if they are suffering from mental health problems.[10] Participation in such schemes is likely to worsen their mental health in a vicious, downward spiral.

Crypto currencies – rebels and revolution

Cryptos are a whole new lexicon in the ancient language of money.

Bitcoin was invented in 2008 by a person called Satoshi Nakamoto (although some think there's a collective of people behind the invention and no one knows the real identity of the inventor/s).

Bitcoin (and cryptos as a whole) is a combination of computer science (blockchain), economics, philosophy and politics. It was

born out of a collective of cyberpunks and internet rebels with lofty ambitions to create a revolution: to create a cashless society. Bitcoin can appear incomprehensible, as the beleaguered figure in the illustration shows. Just when we think we've fathomed one layer, we're confronted with another.

The best way to understand bitcoin is to look at what it set out to do.

To do that, we need to compare paying for purchases with cash versus paying via third-party mechanisms such as Visa, Amex and so on. The issue here, once again, is trust. If we buy something from a street vendor, say a pound of apples from a farmers' market, both the farmer and we have complete trust in the transaction. We can see the apples we are handed by the farmer who can see the money we give them in exchange. Neither party needs a trusted intermediary in the middle. This is known as 'peer to peer'. It's direct, simple and safe.

But if we are conducting the transaction online, how do we have faith as either a buyer or a seller? How do we know the seller will deliver the goods or that the buyer will pay for them? The answer is both rely on a third party to supervise the transaction: Visa, Amex, Mastercard etc. We send Amex the money, Amex confirms the money has been sent, the vendor sends us the goods, Amex sends the vendor the money. They sit like giant, hungry spiders at the centre of the money web. And, in 2017, the little bites they took from each transaction added up to $1.9 trillion.[11]

And not only that, but despite electronic payments in theory going at the speed of a few keyboard clicks, it often takes days for money to end up in the right accounts. The UK Cards Association reports that in 2016, in the UK alone, we spent £709 billion on credit and debit cards. Globally, in 2017, payment cards were used for purchases amounting to a value of $25.1 trillion.[12] Imagine the interest that can be earned by sitting on these sums of money for a few days.

But the creators of bitcoin thought: what if we step off the existing payment platforms, bypass governments and create a peer to peer payment system, like cash, where someone online can sell to someone else online DIRECTLY, with no third-party oversight, no Amex or Visa creaming off huge fees? What if we create a system where you don't need to trust the other party because the transaction is verified not by one possibly corruptible computer, but by tens, hundreds or thousands of computers via complicated mathematical cryptography using prodigious amounts of energy to verify and prove that the payment has moved from A to B? What if we create an ever-lengthening chain, with new transactions linked to existing ones? A chain that due to the complexity of the maths and the enormous investment of computing energy and time needed to verify each link, and due to the visibility of all the links in the chain to all the participants, is impossible to fake?

That would be worth something wouldn't it? Especially to people who didn't have an Amex card, or didn't have a bank, or lived in a country with a dodgy fiat currency rendered almost worthless by inflation or counterfeiting. That would be worth something to people who couldn't trust their banking system either because of fraud or political interference. Or to people with libertarian or anarchic tendencies, or who just didn't like the financial establishment with its oligopolistic[13] power and its careless disregard for their money.

And so bitcoin was born.

There are a whole host of other crypto currencies too extensive to cover here.

Crypto currencies are like Marmite. People either love them or hate them. They have been described as the democratisation of money or a menace to the world economy. Their death is predicted on an almost daily basis but they rise again these 'zombie' currencies.

Cryptos are a strange hybrid. They are not money, but they can fulfil some of the functions of money, such as acting as a medium of exchange with which you can buy things (not very many things as of 2020). They are, in part, a speculative asset, bought in the hope that their price will rise, which, sometimes, and for a while, it can and does. But it can also fall, dramatically. The value of cryptos is highly volatile. Fortunes can be made, and lost.

Will cryptos ever become mainstream? Will they ever replace fiat money? Look at the internet. When it was first created critics said it would be the domain of paedophiles and other criminals. The first emails had to be written in code and took three days to arrive. After two decades, the internet has evolved into a highly accessible ubiquitous good many of us enjoy, use with ease and take for granted. By 2040, the same might just be true of cryptos, especially for the children of today. Their morning croissant, their journey to work, their grocery shopping might be paid for with cryptos. In the meantime, as of 2018, several Premier League football clubs were considering plans that would enable fans or speculators to buy Cardiff City or Newcastle United cryptos. A whole new Premier League of cryptos will evolve over time. But as with football, backing the winners is never as easy as it seems.

One thing is certain, however. The financial technology ('fintech') upon which cryptos are based is here to stay. It has led to what

Anne Boden, the founder and chief executive of Starling Bank, has called the Money Revolution.[14]

In short

For the financially adventurous, cryptos can be an interesting investment if you have money to burn. Electronic money is supremely useful, particularly in times of pandemics, but using it can warp our spending decisions. Cash is in danger of dying a slow death (hastened by coronavirus), yet it still fulfills a multitude of important roles.

If we want to reduce our spending and save more, we should switch wherever possible to using cash instead of payment cards. And we should always keep a readily available stash of cash to hand in case of technological meltdown in banking systems or hacking. If we care about cash and those who rely upon it, we should fight for its preservation.

Chapter Four

How to multiply money
– the eighth wonder of the world

So that's a look at a sliver of the big picture of money, its history and where it's going. But what of personal money? What of the money in our pockets and our bank accounts? How can we grow that? How can we facilitate our dreams of buying a property, of retiring early, of making money work for us, rather than vice versa?

The answer is to understand the theoretical concept known as *time value of money*. And to put this to practical effect by investing. Start now. Even better, start young. Why? Because of a particular kind of financial alchemy which Einstein called 'the eighth wonder of the world': *compound interest – earning interest on interest or returns on returns.*

My favourite example involves Manhattan. Before it was acquired by the British in exchange for a nutmeg-producing island called Run, it was sold in 1626 by Native Americans to Peter Minuit for trinkets and beads worth about $26 dollars. Had the Native Americans been able to invest this in a savings account at an 8 per cent interest rate, or in the stock market and reap an average 8 per cent return annually, reinvesting all their income or dividends, they and their descendants could have sat back in the intervening centuries and watched their savings grow to $384 trillion. Easily enough to buy back Manhattan.

You might say that, while this all sounds fine in theory, in practice, you have neither hundreds of years nor large sums of money to play with. But you don't need to start with a fortune. If you can buy a cappuccino every day then you're rich enough to invest. Small savings can grow into substantial sums if you invest regularly and you start young.

And you don't need to be Methuselah either. The power of compounding is such that you can reap great rewards in surprisingly short periods of time.

Let's say you forego your daily £3.50 cappuccino and invest the money instead in a low-cost diversified equity fund.[1]

What would you say if I told you that in thirty years' time you could have a portfolio worth £105,000?

Here's the maths:
- Monthly savings: £105
- Investment frequency: monthly
- Annual return: 6 per cent
- Value in thirty years: £105,474

Let's change the model slightly to show the power of regular investing. Let's assume that instead of investing £105 every month you filled a jam jar until you had an annual pot of £1,260 and you invested that once a year for thirty years.

The future value comes out at £99,613. So you lose out on roughly £6,000 just because you invested annually rather than monthly.

Another refinement: let's say you free up £5 a day by foregoing your daily pain au chocolat along with your cappuccino, and invest £150 a month for thirty years at an annual rate of return of 6 per cent.

In thirty years you would have a nest egg worth £150,677.

If you manage to pump that interest rate up to an annual 8 per cent, your nest egg will be worth a staggering £224,000.

At 9 per cent annual compounding, you'd receive £274,611.

Of course, there are periods when the stock market grows on average by less than 6 per cent per annum and it can and does go down in value. Sometimes dramatically. Coronavirus, with all its tragic consequences for health and life itself, has sickened financial markets too: in early 2020 markets have shown sharp collapses and feverish rises. (We will look at this in more detail in later chapters.) But the effects of such falls are mitigated if you reinvest dividends and are generally more than made up for if you are able to invest for the long term, as in our examples.

Investing via a stocks and shares ISA can be even more powerful as any gains you make when you sell your portfolio will be tax-free. As of March 2020, the maximum you can invest per annum is £20,000, but you can start an ISA with an initial lump sum of £100, or a monthly investment of £25. The Money Advice Service is an excellent resource which provides free and impartial information on ISAs.

What's fascinating is how quickly you can double your money with annual compounding of interest or investment returns. The banks have a lovely formula that you can use: 'the rule of 70'.

The rule of 70

Divide 70 by the interest (or return) your savings/investments are earning. Let's say it's 3 per cent. Dividing 70 by 3 gives you 23. So, in twenty-three years your initial investment will have doubled. If you're receiving 9 per cent then your money will have doubled in just under eight years.

If you like maths and are as fascinated as I am by compound interest, treat yourself to an HP 12C financial calculator. I was given one when I worked as a leveraged buyout specialist in my first job at Bankers Trust in 1985. I've kept it ever since. You can teach yourself to use it via YouTube tutorials. It shows you graphically and persuasively the benefits of investing and the costs of borrowing (we'll address borrowing later) over time.

Retiring early

The power of compounding and saving is put to work by a movement known as FIRE (Financial Independence, Retire Early). This took off in North America and spread to the UK. Let me give you a real example of an accountant with a partner and three teenage children who retired at the age of 43.

He states that his salary is unexceptional but that he managed to save about 50 per cent of his post-tax income each year. He invested this in low-cost funds that track the stock market and achieved an average return of about 12 per cent a year for nineteen years. Using the rule of 70, that would mean doubling his money in just under six years. In this way, he amassed a pot of £600,000, which gives him and his family £24,000 a year to live on. He speaks of the aggregation of marginal gains, optimising every spending and saving decision over time, which adds up to something amazing and delivers freedom.

One of the greatest investors in our current times, Warren Buffett, estimated that by adjusting the frequency of his haircuts and investing his savings he could net $300,000 over his lifetime, a testament to both the power of compounding and making marginal savings where possible.

The basic mathematics of FIRE is that, to retire, you need to have amassed a nest egg of 25 times your annual spending. Proponents advocate investing your savings sensibly in low-cost funds that track the stock market[2] and/or in buy-to-let property. It assumes a safe withdrawal rate from your fund of 4 per cent each year. If you withdraw any more than that you are in danger of running out of money over the long term. Some commentators argue that a 2 per cent annual withdrawal would be more prudent, meaning that if you wish to have the same retirement income as a 4 per cent withdrawal rate would imply, you'd need to amass a much bigger pot to fund that income (equivalent to fifty times your annual spending requirements).

Most FIRE practitioners stick with the 4 per cent annual safe withdrawal model. So, on this basis, if you're happy to live on £24,000 a year and you have no mortgage, that means that you would need to save a pot of £600,000. Correspondingly, if you need to spend around £50,000 a year you need a pot of £1.25 million. It might sound like a pipe dream but many thousands of individuals and families have saved aggressively, invested wisely and retired early. Barney Whiter, aka the Escape Artist, a FIRE follower who retired in his forties after achieving financial independence, says that once you embark on the FIRE journey, 'You realise it's all about rejecting consumerism. You come for the money and you stay to save the world.'[3] This philosophy and practice helps FIRE practitioners save aggressively, often as much as 50 per cent of their post-tax income.

Yet, alarmingly, one in four British adults has no savings at all according to the Skipton Building Society. The Office for National Statistics reports that the UK savings ratio, which measures total savings as a share of disposable income, fell to a record low of 3 per cent in 2017. More encouragingly, in the second quarter of 2019 it increased to 6.8 per cent. Helen Morrissey, a pensions specialist at Royal London, surveyed 1,500 UK millennials in 2017 and found they were saving on average 4.6 per cent of their income for retirement. 'This is well short of current rules of thumb, which suggest contributions of 12–15 per cent of income are needed.'[4] Whether we want to retire early or not, the message is clear. We need to save more.

In short

Start saving as soon as you can. Ideally, start young. Use tax-efficient ISAs wherever possible. Analyse your spending decisions to see what you can do without and if you can reduce the frequency of regular expenditures. Small changes can make a big difference.

For desperate families saving remains elusive, but if you are able to save and invest just small sums regularly over the long term, because of the wondrous power of compounding you will reap substantial dividends, literally and metaphorically.

Chapter Five

How to invest money

– the stock market, property, liquid assets and reckless conservatism

So, you might ask, into what kind of investment should I put my savings, cappuccino or otherwise?

Realistically there are four categories:

- The stock market
- The property market
- Commodities such as gold, fine wines, whiskies or stamps
- Interest-bearing bank accounts or cash ISAs (these will impoverish you in your old age if you rely on them but for completeness' sake I must include them here as portfolio theory always insists on a cash component)

Professional portfolio managers and financial advisers will always recommend a *diversified portfolio* (i.e. not putting all your eggs in one basket) – which will encompass all of the asset classes above as well as some other asset classes, such as the bond market, which I will not cover here as it is an asset class best left to the professionals for a variety of reasons.[1]

Do I need a financial adviser or can I invest independently?

If you have over £50,000 to invest, then you could approach your bank and ask for their recommendations and/or do your own research to find one. Martin Lewis's excellent MoneySavingExpert website offers a detailed guide to sourcing and researching advisers.[2] Before getting into any conversation with an advisor, use Google to find out as much as you can about them. ALWAYS check they are regulated by the Financial Conduct Authority and find out what fees they are charging for their advice and for the products they are recommending. High fees can erode investment returns. When someone is pushing an investment, ask yourself who benefits and by how much? Beware of those who use jargon and can't explain things simply, like the city slicker opposite.

Going it alone

You can invest in all the sectors above independently, with sums from £25 a month upwards. I will show you how in this chapter and at various stages throughout this book, and recommend sites where you can find more detailed information.

Let's look at how the three main asset classes – shares, property and cash – have performed over time and at how you can invest in each.

If you examine the table on page 40 you can see that investors in shares who consistently reinvested all of their dividends (so that compounding might work at its full power) did best over the twenty nine years (up to 2014), earning a total return over that period of 1,433 per cent, which works out as an average annual return of 9.9 per cent.[3]

So, Butterworth Minor, if I have six put options on collateralised front loaded CCOs, should I affirm or unwind my position?

1985–2014	Return in 2014	Sum Invested	% Change	Annualised
Halifax Residential House Price series	£502,455	£100,000	402%	5.7%
UK Equities (Total Return)	£1,533,381	£100,000	1433%	9.9%
UK Equities (capital only)	£532,990	£100,000	433%	5.9%
UK RPI	£267,430	£100,000	167%	3.5%
Base Rate (reinvesting interest)	£538,549	£100,000	438%	6.0%
Base Rate (interest only)	£275,500	£100,000	176%	3.6%

If you had taken all your dividends as cash and spent them instead of reinvesting them in the stock market your returns would have dropped to 433 per cent or an annual rate of 5.9 per cent. That is actually worse than you would have got if you had put them in a cash savings account, where you would have made a total of 438 per cent over the period – equivalent to an average of 6 per cent per annum. Property was the worst performer over this period, with a total return of only 402 per cent, but that is misleading, because if you restricted your analysis to the latter part of this time period, when house price inflation went crazy, stats would show it outperformed the stock market and bank savings deposits (see data below).[4] This reveals an important lesson: you can often make statistics show what you want them to depending on what you measure and over what time period.

Unfortunately, in our current monetary era, those who keep their savings in cash will not see their money grow. In real terms, they will actually see the purchasing power of their money shrink. By May 2020, Halifax, NatWest, Santander and Lloyds were all offering savers 10 pence a year for each £1,000 deposited with them. With retail price inflation running at 2.6 per cent, that would erode the real value of these deposits (what they can actually buy) by £259 in a single year.

2000–2014	Return in 2014	Sum Invested	% Change	Annualised
Halifax Residential House Price series	£231,873	£100,000	132%	5.8%
UK Equities (Total Return)	£182,659	£100,000	83%	4.1%
UK Equities (capital only)	£112,273	£100,000	12%	0.8%
UK RPI	£153,616	£100,000	54%	2.9%
Base Rate (reinvesting interest)	£151,590	£100,000	52%	2.8%
Base Rate (interest only)	£142,500	£100,000	43%	2.4%

How to invest in the stock market

You can invest in stock market funds with as little as £25 a month.[5] You can invest up to £20,000 annually via ISAs, where both your capital and dividends will be tax-free. Beyond that, you can invest as much as you like. But non-professionals tend not to like.

During the UK tax year to April 2018, we set up almost three times as many cash ISAs as stock market ISAs (7.8 million versus 2.8 million). But over 2017, consumer price inflation averaged 2.74 per cent, which means it was three times as high as the average cash ISA rate of return of 0.93 per cent. The real value of our ISA – what it would actually buy us – was shrinking before our eyes. In contrast, the average stocks and shares ISA returned growth of 11.75 per cent.[6]

So why do we overwhelmingly choose cash? What lies behind this seemingly illogical choice?

To understand, let's take a closer look at the upsides and the downsides of the equity markets and see how they scar our subconscious and distort our decisions.

Bull markets, bear markets, volatility and time horizons

The thing that puts many people off from investing in the stock market is that prices can fall as well as rise. Market professionals call this *volatility*. We have seen dramatic stock market rises and falls as a result of the coronavirus pandemic. In March 2020 there have been *daily* falls (and partial bouncebacks) in major stock market indices of over 5 per cent, sometimes over 10 per cent. Since its peak of 7,877 in May 2019, the UK FTSE 100 (the index of the one hundred largest companies quoted on the London Stock Exchange) has fallen by over 36 per cent and, in late March 2020, was hovering around 5,000. That's enough to terrify most people, including many market professionals. Anyone who has to sell shares will likely incur a huge loss (unless they bought into the index at the various points when it was below 5,000). The key here is *not to sell*. Historic data shows that if you can avoid selling you will prosper over the medium term, especially if you reinvest your dividends. Annabel Brodie-Smith of the Association of Investment Companies[7] points out that, if you had invested £1,000 in an average investment trust immediately before the stock market crash of 2008 and held onto it, as of Friday 13 March 2020 it would have grown in value to £2,348. Markets recover, if we can wait. But, crucially, we must have the ability to wait.

Let's take a look at how the FTSE has risen and fallen over thirty-five years to 2020 as shown in the table[8] below.

Year	Index	% change
19 March 2020	5,052	-31.5
2 December 2019	7,380	9
2018	6,728	-12.5
2017	7,688	7.6
2016	7,143	14.4
2015	6,242	-4.9
2014	6,566	-2.7
2013	6,749	14.4
2012	5,898	5.8
2011	5,572	-5.6
2010	5,900	9.0
2009	5,413	22.1
2008	4,434	-31.3
2007	6,457	3.8
2006	6,221	10.7
2005	5,619	16.7
2004	4,814	7.5
2003	4,477	13.6
2002	3,940	-24.5
2001	5,217	-16.2
2000	6,223	-10.2
1999	6,930	17.8
1998	5,883	14.5
1997	5,136	24.7
1996	4,119	11.6
1995	3,689	20.3
1994	3,066	-10.3
1993	3,418	20.1
1992	2,847	14.2

1991	2,493	16.3
1990	2,144	-11.5
1989	2,423	35.1
1988	1,793	4.7
1987	1,713	2.0
1986	1,679	18.9
1985	1,413	14.7

The data shows that every year is different, often alarmingly so. There are ups and downs all over the place. There are multiple bull markets – defined by rising stock markets and a feeling of optimism – and many corrections (falls of more than 10 per cent) and bear markets (falls of more than 20 per cent).

Most commentators would argue that, because they weren't halted by a bear market, the main stock markets have been in a continuous bull run since 2009, despite blips in 2011 and 2015 and a bigger blip in 2018. This bull run was comprehensively ended by coronavirus in March 2020, which has seen stock market falls of over 30 per cent.

How can anyone on the outside manage to understand these rises and falls, let alone predict them? I have to add, often, many of those on the inside cannot and do not.

But the reality is it doesn't matter. *You don't need to understand it.* You *do* need to invest in a fund managed actively by a good fund manager or in an indexed tracker fund and to do so for long enough to ride out the volatility, holding on to your stock during bear markets so you can take advantage of the bull markets. The average annual rise between 1985 and the end of 2019 was 6.3 per cent per annum and that's without reinvesting dividends, which would have bumped the return up considerably.

Don't try and game the markets over shorter periods by buying and selling. The old investors' axiom 'time in the market beats timing the market' is a sound one.

Do re-invest dividends. Let me give you another example of the power of reinvesting dividends and how it can protect you against stagnant markets.

On New Year's Eve 1999, the FTSE 100 closed at a then record high of 6,930. If you had invested £1,000 at that time then sat on it, by 14 December 2018 it would have been worth £993 without reinvesting dividends. (That's not adjusting for the effects of inflation or charges.) However, if you had opted to reinvest the dividends paid by the index's listed companies, your investment would have been worth £1,935 by December 2018. That's an annual return of 3.54 per cent compared with –0.04 per cent if you had invested in the index alone.[9]

The financial community loves acronyms and refers to dividend reinvestment schemes as DRIPs. Don't be put off. Tick that box!

What is an actively managed fund and how do I invest in one?

Actively managed funds are run by individuals who use their expertise to assess the performance history and prospects of markets and companies and use this to select a range of investments designed to optimise their investment strategy. This strategy might be to aim for high-dividend payments, or for capital protection in turbulent times, or for steady capital growth, or for higher (but potentially more risky) capital growth. Equity funds (some of which will have holdings in cash and/or bonds as well) try to outperform the index over time.

To pick a fund, analyse the performance of various fund managers in specific types of funds, say smaller UK companies or more dynamic UK companies, or global trends, and invest in these specific funds (always using as much as possible of your ISA allowance). If you want to diversify even more, pick a spectrum of different funds with good historic and potential future performance. Get googling. Read up, compare the performance of a fund versus its benchmark[10] and over time. Find out what fees they charge and compare the size of their assets under management (AUM). Other things being equal, big is better here. Check how long the particular fund manager/s have been in place. Read up on their investment philosophies and strategies to see if they chime with yours and with what you are looking for. Take your time. There are various online publications which can be helpful in familiarising you with the investing world and what to look for. See the section on 'Useful resources' at the end of this book.

In making your investment choices, give some thought to what is referred to as 'the triple bottom line' and environmental, social and governance issues.

The triple bottom line was conceived in 1994 by John Elkington, a British management consultant and sustainability guru. He added *people* and *planet* to the conventional yardstick by which companies are judged – *profit*. The aim is to improve people's lives and the planet while also making a profit. Using this measure of a company's performance might nudge us to invest in such companies, to seek to work for them and to buy from them, all of which will help them prosper, potentially at the expense of those companies who ignore or downplay people and planet. In this way, the power of capitalism can be harnessed for the general good.

This forms part of the broader umbrella of what is known as environmental, social and governance (ESG), the three essential factors used to measure the sustainability and social impact of an investment in a company or business. A growing number of institutional investors make decisions based on ESG considerations among others.[11] There are now ESG rating agencies which measure companies' commitment to ESG issues and practical action taken. This can help both institutional and individual investors choose which companies to invest in and which companies to shun. In this way, you can build your nest egg in an ethical manner.

What is a tracker fund and how do I invest in one?

Index trackers are financial instruments you buy from a fund company which aim to mirror the performance of an index either by buying a range of investments in that index or via more complicated instruments. The Money Advice Service has a liferaft of excellent information.[12]

Trackers can be useful vehicles but they are not without problems.

Trackers are known as *passive* investments. Specific shares are not *actively* chosen by a manager because s/he thinks they are a good bet. They're bought or sold simply according to a mathematical formula that calculates their weight in an index or benchmark.

This means that money flows in to stocks that are rising relative to others, thereby potentially creating a bandwagon effect and the same in reverse.[13] By contrast, active managers will try to find less loved shares which offer greater potential for rises in the future, and will tend to sell off shares that have done very well so far, potentially exhausting their upward climb relative to others.

Passive investments change the structure of markets. Research suggests that once the proportion of passive funds exceeds half the market, share prices become more sensitive to flows rather than fundamental considerations of what they are really worth. Call this a financial version of style over substance.

In general, a well-managed *actively* managed fund with competitive fees is far superior to a *passive* tracker index. But trackers are better than a bad fund manager. If you're not confident that you can identify a good fund manager then choose a tracker.

Robinson Crusoe investing

If you have short-term cash requirements the equity market is not for you. However, if you have a time horizon greater than five years, and some would argue greater than three years, the equity markets are much more suitable. Stick your investment away, select automatic reinvestment of all dividends to supercharge the compounding effect, and forget about it. This is known as the *Robinson Crusoe* approach. Invest money in anticipation of being marooned for years on a desert island with no electronic devices. Whilst you're stranded your investment can do its own thing and grow, unimpeded, for you. And, if you invest in the UK via an ISA, gains and dividend reinvestments are tax-free. You don't even need to trouble your island idyll by worrying about the taxman.

Reckless conservatism

So why don't we do this? Why is the allure of cash so powerful when it can impoverish us? Why do we shun the equity markets when they would enrich us?

The answer is fear and a lack of understanding. Crashing markets make newspaper headlines that sear our subconscious and warp our conscious decision-making. We are guided by the latent fear that if we ever invested our money in the markets we could lose everything or, at the very least, impoverish ourselves. We don't understand the markets or, often, how to invest in them. We are scared of them, so we stick to cash. Which we think is safe.

But there are considerable risks to keeping your money in cash.

Those who put most of their long-term money into cash or interest-bearing deposits rather than the equity market are guilty of what is referred to as 'reckless conservatism'. Their extreme aversion to risk actually makes more likely the outcome they fear: impoverishment in their old age. First, because interest rates are at all time lows (going negative in some countries – i.e. YOU have to pay the bank to hang on to your money for you). Second, because inflation, albeit at currently very low levels, is eating away the real purchasing power of cash (as we saw earlier in this section). In contrast, historic stock market rates of return have, usually, comfortably exceeded inflation, preserving and growing the real value of investments, giving you more of a buffer to see out your old age.

Property

You can invest in property in two main ways.

Indirect property investments. You could buy shares in property companies listed on indexes or you could buy investment trusts which invest in a range of property assets via real estate investment trusts (REITs).[14] One way of investing in property that is probably best avoided is via open-ended funds,[15] which can be very hard to liquidate for cash under certain circumstances.

Direct property investments – buying your own home or a buy-to-let property. If you are able to borrow money to finance your home or a buy-to-let property at a lower interest rate than the prevailing rate of inflation of property prices then, over time, you will do very well. This is the power of *leverage*.

Leverage

Time for some more maths. Let's say you managed to buy a tiny studio in Hampstead for £100,000 today, putting down a lump sum of £30,000 and borrowing £70,000 for 30 years at a 5 per cent rate of interest. Let's say that the average annual rate of increase in property prices in Hampstead is 9 per cent[16] and that your monthly borrowing and repayment cost will be £376.[17] After 30 years you will have paid a grand total of £135,279 (£70,000 repayment of principal plus total interest of £65,279). That sounds like a lot of interest, but it's a very good investment given the end value of the studio, which, after 30 years, will be worth a staggering £1,326,767.

So, deducting the £135,279 you spent on your mortgage and the original down payment of £30,000, you will be sitting on a gain of £1,161,489. All from being able to exploit a positive difference between borrowing costs and house price inflation and from being able to apply leverage to your cash lump sum.

However, as a result of the global financial crisis in 2008–09 (and, more recently, as a result of coronavirus and its effects upon the economy), it is now more difficult to get a mortgage and you need to put down a higher deposit than used to be the case. To add insult to injury, as a result of the quantitative easing used by central banks in response to the 2008–09 crisis (and on an ongoing basis since then), property prices have risen stratospherically in most locations in the United Kingdom, so you need to have saved up a tidy lump sum before you can buy, as many frustrated buyers know all too well.

Gold

Gold has remained a very popular means of saving and investing. Thousands of years of history and mythology have lent gold a gravitas and credibility that investors turn to in uncertain times. High proportions of central bank reserves in developed countries are invested in gold.[18] When central banks were asked by the gold dealer BullionStar why they held gold, they invariably answered as a war chest or safe haven in times of crisis.[19]

If you live in a country where you don't trust the fiat currency and/ or you don't trust banks, you might also put your savings into gold. Large-scale money managers investing other people's money will often have a component of their portfolio invested in gold and, if they fear political or economic turmoil on the global stage, they will increase the percentage of their portfolio invested in the precious metal.

You can see the effects of such global fears when the gold price ratchets up dramatically, as it has a habit of doing. The global economic crisis in 2008–09 triggered a rise in the price of gold over the following four years of over 250 per cent.[20]

There are four main ways to buy gold or get exposure to gold.

Gold bars – bullion

These are a thing of beauty. Go and visit the Bank of England's museum and take a look at their lustrous gold bars. It's the closest most of us will ever get to one. A standard gold bar, known as a 'Good Delivery' bar (meaning it meets stringent criteria set to ensure the highest quality of bullion production), is 12.5 kilos of pure 24-carat gold. When I was finishing an earlier draft of this book in May 2018, it was worth £388,403. Completing another draft in November 2019, it had risen 23 per cent to £480,609. (This rise is largely due to an increase in perceived political, geostrategic and equity market uncertainties on a global level. Investors flock to gold when they get nervous. It has always been seen as the gold-standard investment and protection against uncertainty.) As of 18 March 2020, in the midst of the coronavirus pandemic and market turmoil, the price of a Good Delivery bar has risen still further to £536,251.

However, there are much cheaper ways of buying gold which bring with them tax advantages.

Gold coins

You could buy gold coins. Any gains you make are tax-free, which makes gold coins an attractive investment in more ways than one. Capital gains tax is not levied on any British currency, and gold sovereigns, gold Britannia coins and silver Britannia coins are all regarded as currency. However, gold bars, as they are not deemed currency, are liable for capital gains tax. The effective price per ounce of sovereigns is slightly higher than for gold bars but this is more than compensated for by the tax break over the long term.

Investing in a fund that invests in gold

For most investors, the cheapest way to invest in gold is through exchange-traded funds (an investment that tracks the price).[21] They can be bought through brokers and most fund platforms.[22]

Investing directly in companies that mine gold

This is a riskier method as you will be exposed to the efficiency and profitability of the company concerned, but it can also lead to potentially higher returns when the gold price rises. If high-adrenaline investing is your thing and if you feel able to analyse individual companies well then this may be the method for you (see Chapter Nine, which explores the relationship between money and psychology).

But, like many commodities, gold can be volatile – its price can rise and fall dramatically and it can also fall out of fashion as an asset class, which can lead to lengthy spells in the price doldrums, as we shall see when we take a peek at 'Brown's Bottom' in Chapter Six: 'How to lose money'.

Alcoholic investments

You can also invest tax-free in alcohol. I copied the information below from an advertisement encouraging people to invest in whisky in the barrel:

What the advert means by *liquid* is that you can buy or sell it easily. Casked whisky would appear to be liquid in two senses – see illustration opposite. Shares in FTSE 100 companies are liquid too (you could pick up a phone to a broker or sell them online in seconds). But you can't drink them. Property is an *illiquid* investment because you can't sell a house in a hurry.

... hic ... did yoush know thaa wishky ish a ... hic ... liquid ashhet?

Wines can also be an attractive liquid investment. Miles Davis of Wine Owners, a fine wine trading exchange, says, 'Tracking the prices of the 250 best wines since 2007, we found they rose by 11 per cent a year, far outstripping more conventional investments.'[23]

It's long since gone out of fashion, but collecting stamps can be a lucrative pastime. Have a dig in the attic. You might just find the stamp collector's holy grail: the Penny Black. Over the decade to 2015, prices nearly tripled – a compound annual growth rate of 11.4 per cent.[24]

Caveat emptor, or buyer beware

Unfortunately, a large number of scammers offer fraudulent investments, most of which appear online. They claim to be regulated by the Financial Conduct Authority (FCA), they steal the logos of reputable firms and even the photographs of known experts, and they masquerade as the real deal. A recent investigation by *The Times* newspaper[25] found a number of fraudulent websites offering cash ISAs promising returns of 9 per cent. Given that most cash ISAs offer returns of 1 per cent, this is an extraordinary proposition and should sound a deafening warning bell. If something looks wrong, if it looks too good to be true then it almost certainly is. The FCA lists fraudulent sites on its scams register (although it can be slow to update its records). It also lists legitimate companies. It should be your first port of call when checking on investment managers. See the 'Useful resources' section for sources of advice on which platforms to choose and which to avoid when investing.

In short

Time horizon permitting, invest in the stock market.

Don't put all your eggs in one basket. Aim for diversity. Buying a low-cost tracker fund will achieve this for you or, even better, buy a fund run by a reputable, reliable, active fund manager who delivers on their promises.

Use tax-free ISAs wherever you can.

Reinvest your dividends.

Be mindful of the impoverishing nature of cash investments. That said, always keep hold of a small stash of physical cash.

If you can, employ leverage (borrowing) judiciously to access and profit from the property market.

Take a look at investing in commodities such as gold.

Do your research and beware of fraudsters.[26]

Check your money psychology and invest accordingly (see next chapters).

If something looks too good to be true, it almost certainly is.

Chapter Six

How to lose money

– 'Brown's Bottom', burning money and vampire notes

I'm not advocating losing money but if I share with you some spectacular ways of doing so it might help you swerve the pitfalls.

Bad timing

One of the best ways to lose money is to get your timing wrong. Typically, people who get their timing wrong are either in a hurry or else their egos are bigger than their brains. Like most things, the price of gold is volatile. If you own gold and wish to sell it, watch your timing.

Brown's Bottom

As of November 2019, the UK had a gold reserve of around 310 tonnes of gold.

We would have more than twice that much but for former Prime Minister Gordon Brown. While still Chancellor, he decided to raid the piggy bank, selling 395 tonnes of gold between 1999 and 2002. He sold this gold at an average price of about US$275 per ounce. This represented the bottom of a thirty-year low in its price. Commentators refer to this as 'Brown's Bottom'.

As of May 2020, the price was $1,693 per ounce. The interim peak was $1,780.65 per ounce.

The moral of this story is get to know your money psychology and behave accordingly (see Chapter Nine).

Inflation

Another terrible way to lose money with devastating personal consequences is to be exposed to inflation, particularly hyperinflation,[1] as we have seen recently in Venezuela and historically and most notably in Germany's Weimar Republic.

One of the consequences of divorcing paper money from the gold that defined its value was inflation (and it is for this reason that hyperinflation is largely but by no means exclusively a twentieth- and twenty-first-century phenomenon).[2] Governments, no longer restricted by the global availability of gold, began to print money. What happens if you increase the notes and coins in circulation is that more money ends up chasing the same amount of goods. This could be food, clothes, machines or houses. The seller quickly realises that they can sell at a higher price. So they do. The apple you bought yesterday for 20 pence now costs 25 pence. That sounds annoying but not catastrophic. But make no mistake, inflation, especially what's called hyperinflation, is like a deadly epidemic, destroying and disfiguring everything in its path. For most people. But, as with all financial phenomena, there are winners and losers.

Burning money – German inflation between 1914 and 1923

In 1914, on the first day of the First World War, Germany suspended the gold standard to preserve its gold reserves, which would otherwise have run out as people sought to exchange their paper money for gold. The German government began to borrow money from the central bank to fund the war in a process akin to printing money (they planned to repay these loans by expropriating the reserves of countries they aimed to conquer). As this new money flooded into the economy, prices began to rise. At first, the rise was hardly noticeable: an annual rate of increase of between 1 and 2 per cent. But by the end of the war the amount of money in circulation had risen by 400 per cent and prices by 140 per cent. Post-war, the government remained hooked on printing money. By December 1923, the Reichsbank had printed an additional 496.5 quintillion marks, each of which had fallen to one-trillionth of its value back in 1914 when it could be exchanged for gold.[3]

All this extra money fed the fire of inflation until it turned into a raging inferno: when bank notes became worth less than wood they were literally burned in stoves.

Prices doubled every 3.7 days. The annual rate of inflation rose to a mind-boggling 182 billion per cent. The situation got so bad that many Germans decided to emigrate. Stories abound of personal tragedies. One family sold their home to emigrate to America. When they arrived at the port of Hamburg several days later, the money from the house sale was no longer enough to pay for their crossing. It didn't even pay for their tickets back home.

The domestic currency, the mark, was no longer worth the paper it was printed on. To obtain a single US dollar you would have had to hand over 4.2 trillion marks.

Winners – those with foreign currency. If you happened to have dollars you could buy untold riches. A senior official in the German post office stole letters containing foreign banknotes: 1,717 dollars, 1,102 Swiss francs and 114 French francs. He used this foreign currency to buy two houses and a piano for a friend and to make a donation to his church, possibly seeking absolution.

Winners – those who owned gold. Similarly, if you were fortunate enough to own gold, you would have done very well. During this period the price of gold increased 1.8 times faster than the inflation rate,[4] meaning that those lucky enough to own gold would have seen their purchasing power almost double.

Losers – savers and those who had only German marks. Thrifty savers who had for years built up their nest eggs saw them reduced in value to nothing.

Winners – borrowers. In contrast, borrowers saw the value of their obligations reduced to almost nothing. If you had borrowed 2,790 marks in 1914 to buy one kilo of gold, by 1924, if you sold that kilo of gold, you would have earned a trillion times as many marks or, to put it another way, you could have repaid your entire debt with a microscopic sliver of gold and kept almost the entire kilo.

While savers suffered, the profligate profited in a reversal of traditional financial morality. The bigger the debt, the greater the profit. The state had the biggest debts of all, but many private individuals had borrowed heavily to buy houses, construction land or farmland. For them, inflation was a gift.

A wheelbarrow of vampire notes for a loaf of bread

For ordinary individuals, daily life became almost intolerable. A week's pension wouldn't even buy a cup of coffee. A loaf of bread which cost 250 marks in January 1923 cost 200,000 million marks in November 1923. To buy that loaf you would have had to transport the notes to the baker in a wheelbarrow. To lighten the load, the central bank had already issued new, higher denomination notes of 10,000 marks. These were known as 'vampire notes' because they showed an image of a man with what looked like a vampire bite on his neck.

Some of the stories seem almost comical but were anything but to those who lived through them. People collected their wages in suitcases. One person, who left their suitcase unattended, found that a thief had stolen the suitcase but not the money.

A boy who was sent to buy two bread buns stopped to play football and, by the time he got to the shop, the price had gone up, so he could only afford to buy one.

Winners – those who had real, tangible assets you could eat, drink, play or admire. Farmers, for example, did very well out of the crisis. 'They had money to burn, and spent it willy-nilly,' reported the writer Lion Feuchtwanger. 'Farmer Greindlberger drove from the grimy village street of Englschalking to Munich in an elegant limousine complete with a liveried chauffeur, while he himself was dressed in a brown velvet jacket and a green chamois-tufted hat.'[5]

Those who owned diamonds, gold coins, antiques, pianos and paintings also did well. No one trusted cash anymore. People started bartering instead. Doctors were regularly paid in sausages, eggs, coal and other real commodities.

Those who earned salaries survived because they could renegotiate what they were paid on a daily basis. Those with valuable skills like doctors could trade them for goods.

Losers – those on fixed incomes. Pensioners, for example, were often reduced to destitution. One woman sold her house intending to live on the proceeds. A few weeks later, the money from the sale couldn't even buy her a loaf of bread.

Hyperinflation corrupted the way the normally prudent Germans lived. Dance halls and strip clubs opened up in the cities and cocaine sales skyrocketed. People went on wild spending sprees, living for the day knowing that tomorrow their money would be worthless. The illustration on the next page captures the *live for today, tomorrow be damned* excesses.

Hyperinflation caused the greatest redistribution of wealth Germany had ever seen. But many of the winners were those who had already been wealthy. Trust between the state and the individual was destroyed. Most people's life savings were wiped out but the state was able to shrug off its once enormous debts.

The writer Klaus Mann described it as 'the world coming off the rails'.[6] It's no coincidence that Adolf Hitler's rise to power began in November 1923, the high point of Germany's inflationary period.

Hyperinflation isn't something confined to the history books. It left national scars that still shape the German psyche. A primal fear of inflation means that German economists feel more impelled than most to ensure economic stability and control of the money supply.

The spectre of hyperinflation arises whenever governments lose control of their economies.

In short

It's easy to lose money by making poor investment decisions, notably by getting your timing wrong. Get to know your financial psychology and *behave accordingly before you act* (see Chapter Nine).

And, remember, cash isn't always king, notably if your fiat currency is contaminated by inflation or hyperinflation. Money can die. Essential skills – doctoring, plumbing, farming – and real assets – food, a car, a bicycle, chickens, a house, a diamond – will always act as an insurance policy. As will gold[7] and foreign currency from countries with a healthy financial system.

Chapter Seven

How to steal money
– buying time, multiple shades of grey, naughty money and castration

Again, I'm not advocating stealing money, but the favoured methodology used by those who do can teach us a valuable lesson: the playing field is not level. Mind how you play.

They mug so elegantly, the financially literate. They have no need of the glinting knife or the raised fist. How do they do it? Sometimes downright illegally, sometimes more insidiously in the grey areas where the law is unclear. Financial institutions love to play in the grey areas for it is here that fortunes (of dubious legality) can be made. They call it pushing the envelope.

Stealing time

Time is money. If you can get financial information faster than the next trader, you can make that pay.

The trader's maxim is buy low, sell high. But there's money to be made in stealing almost infinitesimal slices of time for this can enable you to buy low and sell for just a tiny bit more elsewhere (basically before the first party gets the information that the price they sold at should have been higher). This process is known as *arbitrage* and it is predicated on *latency time* (the time it takes between a signal being sent and received) and is facilitated by machines.

Latency time is measured in milliseconds or nanoseconds. These slivers of time are too small for humans to exploit. But not machines. More than 50 per cent of all equity trading in the US is high-frequency trading via computers.

A company called Spread Networks has spent around $300 million building a fibre-optic link through the Appalachian Mountains between New York and Chicago (the old link went around them). The new, shorter cable cut the data transmission time by about a millisecond. Doesn't sound like much, but given the enormous volume of trades the high-frequency machines execute, tiny fractions add up to a huge amount. You couldn't justify spending $300 million on a faster route if they didn't.

This *buying of time* has undermined one of the basic premises of markets – that they be democratic: that the playing field be even, that everyone sees the same thing at the same time. It is effectively a form of insider trading. Insider trading is of course meant to be illegal. This is one of those wonderful grey areas.

Getting news ahead of the rest of the market, *buying time*, and trading on that news at the expense of the market, has been used throughout history as a way to make money.

My favourite example involves pigeons. The following financial tale is arguably apocryphal. I include it to illustrate an essential truth about the value of obtaining information ahead of the market.

Nathan Rothschild and the Battle of Waterloo

The British general Wellington defeated the French general Napoleon at the Battle of Waterloo in 1815. Immediately, a carrier pigeon winged its way across the channel to London where the Rothschild family was waiting.

'Wellington won, Napoleon lost', read the pigeon's note. Before anybody else knew the result of the battle, the Rothschilds supposedly got ready to sell French government bonds and buy British government bonds. But in a spectacularly clever and ballsy twist, Rothschild first did the opposite. Aware that everyone knew of his superior information networks, he strode around the exchange floor selling British bonds and buying French. Panicking holders of British bonds assumed that Britain had lost and France won. Accordingly, they sold British bonds, driving down their price, and bought French bonds, driving up their price.

And then, quietly, unknown agents of the Rothschilds went around the market buying the British government bonds and selling the French ones.

As soon as the real result filtered out, the price of French government bonds fell considerably and the price of British government bonds rose considerably. A combination of knowledge and time landed the Rothschilds a fortune and averted potentially heavy losses – and all via a process that would have been entirely legal at the time.

Different perceptions make a market. Back then, falsely influencing those perceptions was not a crime. Today, the UK's Financial Conduct Authority might make two cases against Rothschild: the first for insider trading (trading on information not available to all the market simultaneously) and the second for market manipulation/abuse.

But it was only in 1985 that the Company Securities (Insider Dealing) Act deemed the practice of trading on information not available to everybody else a criminal offence punishable by prison time.

Trouble is, there remain so many grey areas that can be exploited in return for a fortune. Here's another grey area.

Inside knowledge, hedge funds and the Brexit referendum

Bloomberg reported in June 2018 that in the run-up to the 2016 UK referendum on whether to stay or leave the European Union, hedge funds[1] hired leading UK pollsters to provide private exit polls (predictions of the result) and other data on voter behaviour. Some of this data would have been illegal to give to the general public while voting was underway but no laws restricted the data from being passed on to financial institutions for their trading activities while the polling booths were open.

Once the booths had closed, exit polls could be published. However, it would appear that certain hedge funds had already built up trading positions based on their prior knowledge of these exit polls. After the information became public, the markets moved and the hedge funds cleaned up.

Their prior knowledge had allowed them to take an almost guaranteed bet. The point is, this prior knowledge was price-sensitive information, normally illegal to act upon.

The question is whether or not this activity should be covered by market abuse legislation.

The answer is: *grey area.*

These people were, arguably, stealing value, stealing money.

How to protect yourself

What does all this mean for me and you, the person on the street? It means that taking decisions based on trying to guess a near-time outcome is unwise and to be avoided, as the one thing you can be sure of is that the professionals, the financial sophisticates, what I call 'the legal insiders', will have more and better information than you.

I should know, because I was one of them. I used to work in the heart of the money machine, on one of the biggest trading floors in the City of London. I hasten to add that even when you are operating on completely legal information, you are still on the inside and you still know things that outsiders do not know. This is market sentiment: something as nebulous as the atmosphere on the floor and the emotion of the market participants. These intangible moods will have a very tangible impact on prices. If you are good at reading these, especially when they are subtle and nascent, if you are a kind of market 'empath', then you can and will make a fortune by applying this knowledge to your buying and selling decisions. None of this matters over the longer term, when the fundamental values will assert themselves, but, in the short term, if you are trying to play the timing game and you are not on the inside, unless you are very, very good you are going to lose.

When I left the money machine to write my first book, aptly named *Nest of Vipers*, (inspired by my life on the inside!), I decided that I would not do any more short-term investing but that I would invest and, like Robinson Crusoe, pretend I was on a desert island and sit back and leave my investments alone for years to let them do their thing (unless in individual cases the fundamentals changed, making the company look a poor bet in the long term). What I did not do, was buy and sell, sell and buy on a monthly, weekly, or let alone, on a daily basis. On the outside, I had no chance of *feeling* market sentiment – leave that to the insiders, legal and grey.

So what of the illegal grey areas? Forget fifty shades, there are thousands.

We've seen above the quasi-legal grey areas, but there are many more outright illegal ones. as well as others where the law hasn't yet been framed to catch the ingenious financial crimes being committed which, until they are discovered, remain grey, sort of legal or where the crimes are so well hidden by complexity and volume that they stay hidden. They would be illegal if anyone ever discovered them, but the chances of that can be miniscule. Think of this as the perfect financial crime.

I know this because I have spent many years dreaming them up.

As well as advising official bodies on what to look out for, I have spent many years inventing financial crimes in order to write about them in my thrillers. I value my sleep too much to actually commit them but I do know how easy it would be to do so. And if I know that then rest assured, there will be lots of criminals out there, in sleek suits, putting their own nefarious schemes into practice. Some of these will be aimed at financial institutions, some will be aimed at you and me.

So, how do we protect ourselves from them?

So I asked the MD if we should go long on the double A front loaded credit default swap collateralised options ... and the damned fool didn't know what I was talking about.

These financial sharks like to operate in the grey area of confusion. They often offer investments which are difficult to understand. They play off our desire to be seen as knowledgeable and not reveal that we don't understand something. Financial fraud within banks has been facilitated by both the actual complexity of financial instruments and by deliberate obfuscation, which veils the thieving nicely. Even sophisticated financial insiders do not like to admit when they don't understand something. Fraudsters exploit this – see illustration on previous page. Don't allow yourself to be sucked into this. If someone cannot explain something clearly to you it means either a) they don't understand it themselves or b) they don't actually want *you* to understand it. Either way, run a mile. Also run a mile if something or someone is offering a scheme which offers much higher returns than comparable schemes, like the internet merchants offering cash ISAs or mini bonds with 8 per cent interest. Scammers also tend to market their wares as 'risk-free'. The rule of thumb is that higher rates of return typically come with higher rates of risk. If something looks too good to be true, it almost certainly is!

Stick to the transparent, the simple, the comprehensible, the reputable, the verified, the reasonable and the regulated.

Other ways of stealing money

From time immemorial, way before the advent of high-frequency trading machines, hedge funds, financial insiders and scammers, people were stealing value by fiddling with physical money.

Throughout history, this has been a common pursuit indulged in by the high and the low, by royalty and by their desperate subjects at the bottom of the pile.

The high

Henry VIII (1491–1547) was a faker. His penchant for personal overspending on palaces and parties and public overspending on wars put severe strain on state coffers. Henry had a two-pronged solution: dissolve the monasteries and sell off the loot, basically a form of mugging; and debase the coinage – stealing by sleight of hand. His debasement took three forms:

1 He 'cried up' the currency, switching existing coins for new ones with the same value of metal in them but stamped with a higher face value
2 He minted new coins with the same face value as the older ones they replaced but smaller in size (as chocolate manufacturers like to do today when the cost of cocoa rises)
3 He reduced the metal value of new coins of the same size whilst retaining their face value

In seven years Henry cut the silver content of English coins by more than 80 per cent. The new coins were mainly made of copper alloy but Henry had another trick to try to fool the public. From 1546 he had them 'blanched' by applying a thin coat of pure silver. It didn't fool the public for long. The silver quickly wore off, earning Henry the nick-name 'old copper nose'.

His kingly manoeuvres inevitably backfired as the purchasing power of the coins fell to their new, lower intrinsic value.

The low

The populace were avid fakers too, despite harsh penalties if caught. Historically, those found guilty were castrated or hanged. In 1124,

Henry I, in stark contrast to his sixteenth-century namesake, attempted to preserve the integrity of his coins and the trust in the currency against the depredations of his moneyers – those who minted his coins. He summoned them to an inquest, challenged their methods, found them wanting, and decreed that two-thirds of them have their right hand chopped off. For good measure, he also had them castrated.

Leaping forward again to the era of Henry VIII, perhaps encouraged by their sovereign's antics, a new generation of corrupt moneyers persisted in using short measures, while coin clippers snipped off slivers of metal and counterfeiters faked coins from cheaper metals. This resulted in a great deal of what contemporary reports referred to as 'noythy [naughty] money' circulating through the economy.

This naughty money was no laughing matter. It led to the breakdown of commerce and imperilled civil society. Barter began to replace the fiat currency. No one trusted coins any more. People didn't want to receive them. Nor could they spend them unless willing to pay shopkeepers inflated prices to compensate for the risk of accepting debased coins. Workers' weekly pay became almost worthless. Daily riots ensued. Despite the prospect of hanging if caught, the clippers and counterfeiters continued their desperate trade. In London, hundreds of men and women living in the squalid backstreets known as the Liberties risked freedom and life itself for a few pennies.

In came Henry's daughter, Elizabeth I (1533–1603), who was determined to reform and rehabilitate the currency by a process of recoinage, calling back the debased coins and issuing new ones. This was a Herculean task, beset by problems. In the foreground, charged with creating and distributing these new coins, stood the Royal Mint.

It was ninety-three years after Elizabeth's death that the most striking innovations of the Mint were carried out, under the guiding influence of a surprising source. In 1696, into the Royal Mint walked a workaholic genius best known for his scientific observations on gravity: Sir Isaac Newton.

The Royal Mint – standing on the shoulders of giants

Swearing his oath of allegiance to protect the secrets of the Mint, Newton took up his new position as Warden of the Royal Mint in 1696, subsequently becoming Master of the Mint. He worked with a dedication beyond all the expectations of those who employed him. His aim was to save the coinage, protect it from the clippers and counterfeiters, and improve the efficiency of the production line. He did all this, applying not just the genius of his scientific mind but a prosecutorial zeal that saw him morphing from Cambridge don to private investigator. Seemingly heedless of the dangers, Newton ventured into the hovels, taverns and brothels where the clippers and counterfeiters plied their trade. Recruiting a network of agents in eleven countries, he sleuthed, entrapped, interrogated and pursued the debasers through the mean streets, via the courts, all the way to the Tyburn gallows (present-day Marble Arch).

Newton left the Mint in much better shape than he found it. As well as his war on the debasers, he improved efficiency, business practices and standards of production. The attacks on the coinage continued, as did the attempts of the Mint to outwit them. It's interesting to note that even today counterfeiters are very much alive. The recall of the old one-pound coins in 2017 was in response to one in every thirty – an estimated 45 million coins – being forgeries. The new twelve-sided ones are much harder to counterfeit and are described by the Royal Mint as 'the most secure coin in the world'.

Similarly, technological advances mean that it is now more difficult to counterfeit banknotes in the United Kingdom too. The Bank of England, which is responsible for printing bank notes (De La Rue does the actual physical printing) and maintaining public trust in their integrity, says this:

> The vast majority of counterfeits are discovered before they go back into circulation, when retailers and the banking system are sorting them. A smaller number are detected by the public or retailers who hand them directly to the police, or when the police carry out search warrants. Counterfeits are typically removed from circulation quickly, often after a single use.

> Only a small fraction, typically less than 0.02 per cent of banknotes, are counterfeit, that is less than 1 in 5,000 banknotes. In 2019, around 427,000 counterfeit Bank of England banknotes with a face value of £9.8 million were taken out of circulation. At any one time, there is an average of 3.8 billion genuine banknotes in circulation, with a notional face value of around £75 billion.[2]

In short

The corrupt and ingenious will always find a way to steal money with varying degrees of sophistication. The old-fashioned way to steal money was to fake it, a common pursuit indulged in both by royalty and by their desperate subjects.

Counterfeiting coins and notes is much more difficult today but engaging in financial fraud or what is, at best, sharp practice continues apace. Financial insiders are expert at tilting the playing field in their favour or, to put it another way, exploiting grey areas where the law is unclear. Financial fraudsters also love the world of the grey and the murky.

How can you protect yourself?

Avoid investing in anything that appears too sophisticated, too unclear, has aberrational returns and/or where the person pushing it cannot explain it clearly and simply. If it looks like a gift horse, gallop away. Also, the quick in and out 'day trading' (let alone the second by second trading undertaken by the fast operators) in not a good arena for the layperson. Think slow investing, think Robinson Crusoe. Get money quick more often turns out to be *lose money quick*.

Chapter Eight

Money and children

– how to raise financially literate children and how to invest for them. Angels, demons and gender.

In a world where money can die due to inflation, can be stolen by the financially superliterate and by the cruder counterfeiters, when mis-timing the markets can expose Brown's Bottom, where clambering on to the property ladder seems like an impossible dream, where many young people enter the workplace burdened by heavy student loans, how do we teach our children the language of money?

Too many children grow up knowing little or nothing about how to manage their money and how to avoid money traps. Schools now recognise this and money management is included in the curriculum, but the level of effectiveness varies and time constraints limit the completeness.[1] For large swathes of 2020, coronavirus starved many children of an education of any sort, making their need for financial literacy even more acute.

The girl who mentioned money at the dinner table.

The money taboo

Money is a bigger taboo than sex, religion or politics according to a 2018 YouGov report commissioned by Lloyds Bank. Some 50 per cent of UK adults believe that talking about personal money matters is taboo in everyday conversation – higher than for sex (42 per cent), religion (26 per cent) or politics (14 per cent).

We need to break this taboo. We need to talk about money. For our sakes, and our children's.

Let's start with the mechanics of the first money that children typically get their hands on: pocket money. As I researched this, I discovered some startling differences relating to gender.

Pocket money and gender

The organisation CHILDWISE, which specialises in research on children and young people, reveals both a gender gap in terms of the amount of pocket money received by boys and girls but also a difference in parental attitudes towards the genders.

Every year CHILDWISE conducts research based on online surveys with 2,000 schoolchildren. The 2017 survey showed that boys aged five to sixteen received an average of £10.70 per week from either pocket money, payment for chores or paid work, while girls of the same age received just £8.50. The research showed that the gap widens as the children get older.

CHILDWISE's research manager Jenny Ehren observes that:

The data points towards an early gender imbalance in the way parents educate their children about money matters and financial independence. Boys are more likely to be entrusted with regular cash payments, while girls are more reliant on other people buying them items, or managing money on their behalf. Girls' pocket money is more likely to be supplemented by parents buying expensive items such as clothes and footwear, as well as much cheaper purchases including toiletries and make-up. The value of these purchases almost certainly helps to bridge the income gap between boys and girls, but the approach to managing finances is noticeably different.[2]

Money psychology and gender

Children pick up gender clues all around them, some subtle and some not so subtle. The challenge for parents is to avoid inadvertently perpetuating these gender divisions.

The financial charity MyBnk found that more girls than boys suffered from a crisis of confidence when making money decisions. The charity analysed data on 1,200 people between the ages of 11 and 25 and found that 48 per cent of females felt uneasy talking about finance compared with 20 per cent of males.

A study from the University of Cambridge[3] found that people's financial habits are formed before the age of seven and above the age of three. The Cambridge research found that financial confidence gained then will carry through to adulthood. A study from HSBC of 500 children showed that while 64 per cent of boys are taught by their parents about money, only 54 per cent of girls the same age are. The parents surveyed said they felt more comfortable talking about money to their sons than to their daughters.

Our children, particularly our girls, need to be taught that money is not a dirty word. I'm not advocating that we teach our children to be money hungry or flash. I am advocating that we teach them to understand it.

An interesting side effect of raising the financial literacy of our children is increasing our own too. A pilot course to help parents teach their children about money also improved parents' finances according to the Money Advice Service.[4]

So what should we be teaching our children about money? And what can we do to help provide for them in an era when dizzying property prices, expensive tertiary education, student loans and falling social mobility blight and impoverish so many?

Besides giving them control of their own pocket money and exposing them to what things cost and how to budget, probably the single most important financial lesson we can give our children is the power of compounding.

Financial angels

My advice to adults is to start investing as early as possible. Investing for children in their childhood can be dramatically powerful.

Let's look again at pocket money. Consider the possibility of giving your children half their pocket money in cash and investing the other half for them.

Let's assume the potential investment pot is £5 a week from birth to 18 years of age. Let's further assume you invested it all in a FTSE 100 tracker fund,[5] every month, reinvesting all dividends, at an annual rate of growth of 8 per cent. After eighteen years that modest £5 a week would have grown to a total of £10,403 (£4,680 of that being the total of investments made and £5,723 being the total compounded returns they generated).[6] It's worth noting the power of compounding has made the compounded return alone greater than the total of the monthly pocket money. Even with a much more modest compounding rate of 4 per cent, that weekly £5 would have grown to £6,839 by the time the child is 18.

If the pocket money investment pot were pushed up to £10 a week at a compounding rate of 8 per cent for eighteen years, this would yield £20,803 (£9,360 of pocket money paid in and £11,443 of pure compounded returns). Enough to pay for several years of tuition fees at university or to kickstart a small business. At the more conservative annual growth rate of 4 per cent, the nest egg would still be worth £13,676 in eighteen years' time (£9,360 of pocket money paid in and £4,316 of compounded returns).

It's also possible to invest in a tax-efficient manner via a stocks and shares junior ISA. You can pay up to a maximum of £9,000 per annum into a junior ISA but the minimum investment is £100. The money can be accessed by your child, tax-free, after their eighteenth birthday. Good fund managers will not charge set-up or exit fees on this, making it a particularly attractive means of investing for your child.

Talk to your children about ethical investing, environmental, social and governance (ESG), and the third bottom line. Deploying their money in a way that will help society at large as well as building a nest egg for them can be a powerful motivator. 'Every little helps' is a great slogan to deploy here.

Delaying gratification

It might be worth talking to grandparents about gifting money via investments to their grandchildren instead of buying them endless plastic toys that inevitably end up in landfill. I know this sounds preachy so forgive me, but as children get older they will appreciate gifts of this nature far more and they can also be taught from a surprisingly young age about the virtues of delayed gratification, which essentially gifting cash and saving and investing is all about.

Studies have shown that children who are capable of deferring gratification tend to do better in life, are happier, and are less likely to fall prey to addictions. As the proponents of FIRE (Financial Independence, Retire Early) have shown, restraint rather than consumerism can deliver freedom and can make you captain of your own self rather than indefinitely being a wage slave.

If grandparents prefer something more tangible, then gifts of gold or silver can be both visually and financially pleasing. The Royal Mint makes a fabulous range of gold and silver coins called 'the Queen's Beasts', inspired by the ten heraldic beasts with which Henry VIII lined the bridge over the moat at his Hampton Court Palace. Any gains made on these when sold, as they constitute currency, would also be tax-free.

Financial demons

Leverage: there is good leverage and bad leverage. Good leverage is where you borrow money to buy a house and your rate of interest on the borrowing is lower than the rate of house price inflation (see earlier section in Chapter Five on investing in property).

Leverage can also be applied via student loans, which allow you to undertake a degree which should significantly boost your earnings over time, or not, depending on the nature of the qualification.

But there is bad leverage too, which can blight and destroy lives.

High-interest loans

When we teach children about the positive power of compound interest, we also need to teach them about the destructive negative power of compounding. We can demonstrate that by looking at loans, particularly payday loans or other loans with a high APR.[7]

When you borrow money, interest is calculated for the first period (it could be a day, a week, a month or a year) and is known as *compounding frequency*. (Watch out for this, it makes a HUGE difference to the maths.) This interest is then added to the original total of the money you borrowed (the principal). Interest for the next period is calculated on this new total. So, if you borrow £1,000 over a five-year period and pay a 10 per cent interest rate per annum, the value of the compounding interest and the compound interest added on to your principal will look like this:

Time since loan	Annual interest	Original principal plus cumulative interest
One year	£100	£1,100
Two years	£110	£1,210
Three years	£121	£1,331
Four years	£133.10	£1,464.10
Five years	£146.41	£1,610.51

The total interest paid after only five years would be £610.51.

So after only five years, you will be repaying your initial principal (£1,000) plus more than half as much again (interest £610.51).

Even an interest rate as seemingly innocuous-sounding as 10 per cent per annum is mighty powerful and expensive. But it is dwarfed by the interest charged by payday loan lenders.

Let's say you took out a payday loan of £1,000 on 1 January and repaid it on 1 January the following year. If you borrowed it from one of the payday loan companies that I googled at an APR (annual percentage rate) of 1,325 per cent (yes, you read that correctly), you would need to pay a grand total of £13,250 in interest on top of the original £1,000 loan (for every £1 you borrow you have to pay back £13.25).

That's a disastrous deal for you as a borrower. Loans like this have bankrupted many people. And it's by no means the highest APR out there. Some payday loans charge an APR of 4,000 per cent. That means for every pound borrowed you repay £40 of interest. New laws have been brought in, capping the damage that payday loans can inflict, but they're still out there, still highly toxic to financial health and we need to educate our children about them.

One thing to beware of is that some companies make themselves attractive by seeming to advertise lower interest rates. This is often because they are advertising it for a *shorter period*.

Let me give you a quick example.

Midway through a downpour, your roof collapses. Desperate, you go to a payday lender and they look at your pay stubs and your bank statements and they say, 'OK, we'll lend you £1,000 today and you can repay us in two weeks' time when your salary drops into your bank account. We'll charge you £15 for every £1,000 you borrow.' That's a 15 per cent interest rate, for TWO WEEKS. If you did not repay the £1,000 after two weeks but allowed the debt to rollover for an entire year, with interest compounding every two weeks, the maths would become truly demonic – the APR on 15 % for two weeks is $1.15^{26} - 1 = 3,686$ % pa! The amount you would have to repay at the end of one year would be a staggering, bankruptcy-inducing £37,860.

The other thing we need to educate our children about (and ourselves) is the use and abuse of credit cards. In 2019, according to UK Finance, we owed a collective £72.4 billion on credit cards, an increase of 40 per cent in a decade. The interest alone costs Britons an average of £1,000 a year[8] and one person was declared insolvent or bankrupt every four minutes between July and September 2019.

Gambling, cruel maths and predatory tactics

Another real and growing money menace for children is gambling. This has become particularly pernicious in the internet era due to ease of access and aggressive targeting of children via attractive gaming apps, as well as a less well-known phenomenon called *cruel maths*.

Those who design gaming/gambling software will regularly introduce interactive elements where the online app learns from your gambling predispositions what you are most tempted by and what you are most likely to lose tokens/money gambling or gaming on. They will push these towards you AND they will shift the odds against you, confident you will still be tempted because you are already hooked. It is not a level playing field. The moral of the story is that some fields are best not played on at all.

I can attest to the addictiveness of gambling even back in simpler times (read my intro!). Success sends a lovely shot of dopamine coursing through our veins. And when it wears off, we keep looking for more.

How do children gamble?
Isn't that meant to be illegal?

Yes, but competitive online gamers can bet with virtual items called 'skins' in casino-style sites or on games of luck. Winners can exchange their skins for real currency. Billions of pounds are spent in skin gambling sites internationally and the totals are predicted to rise in coming years. Unlike most regulated online gambling and betting sites, skins gambling sites do not enforce rigorous age verification processes.[9]

Youth gambling is particularly concerning because the young are more susceptible to and more inclined to pursue risk and excitement. Research[10] suggests that adult problem gamblers typically acquire their 'maladaptive patterns' as teenagers. As we've seen earlier, financial habits are formed at an early age.

A report in *The Guardian* in 2018 revealed that 55,000 British 11- to 16-year-olds are classed as problem gamblers – a staggering four hundred per cent increase over the previous two years. Another 70,000 11- to 16-year-olds are considered at risk of becoming problem gamblers. The rate of gambling among young people is higher than that of drinking alcohol, smoking cigarettes or taking illegal drugs. Young men are particularly susceptible. NHS research[11] showed that 1.9 per cent of men between the ages of 16 and 24 were problem gamblers compared with 0.4 per cent of the general population. Not only are boys and young men much more likely to gamble than girls and young women, but multiple studies suggest that they are significantly more likely to be problem gamblers.

The Gambling Commission reported in 2018 that 450,000 11- to 16-year-olds gamble an average of £16 per week (equating to £69.33 per month).

If they invested that monthly over thirty years at a growth rate of 6 per cent per annum, they would have a nest egg of £69,643 in thirty years' time. That's quite a dopamine hit of a good sort.

Dangerous habits – adults and gambling

In 2020, the NHS estimated that more than 400,000 people in England alone have a gambling addiction (meaning the urge to gamble is so intense that it interferes with their daily life and the lives of those around them). Residential hospital stays to treat gambling addiction have doubled in the past six years.

Something about slot machines is particularly addictive. The government calls them a 'social blight' and the 'crack cocaine' of gambling. Gamblers lost £1.82 billion on fixed odds betting terminals (slot machines) in the year to March 2018.

Research commissioned by a leading UK gambling charity, GambleAware, found that problem gamblers were six times more likely to have suicidal thoughts or to try to take their own life – and could be fifteen times more likely to do so.[12]

Nearly one in five, or 19 per cent, had considered suicide in the past year, compared with 4.1 per cent of the general population, while 4.7 per cent attempted suicide, compared with 0.6 per cent in the wider population.

The addictive nature of gambling is made more dangerous still by the exploitative and predatory behaviour of betting firms.

Here's one example. During the coronavirus lockdown, certain betting firms have engaged in predatory tactics to lure reformed gamblers back into the gambling fold, targeting them with thinly-veiled adverts, emails and text messages. Claire Murdoch, the NHS's Mental Health Director, says this: 'As head of England's mental health services and a nurse of 37 years, I am not easily shocked. But reports of firms deliberately targeting ex-punters who have beaten their demons and attempting to exploit them again during coronavirus is below the belt – even for an industry whose moral compass is so consistently off.'[13]

The gambling industry takes upwards of £14 billion a year from punters. Getting to those punters young, via skin games, will add to those profits. This is a case of *moral hazard*. Moral hazard exists when one party gains from engaging in activities which are potentially harmful to another party but does not itself suffer, or share in, the adverse consequences of those actions itself. We'll take a longer look at moral hazard later (see Chapter Ten), but the gambling industry offers a clear example. They have an incentive to create gambling addicts but they do not pay the price of addiction. The addicts and their families do. Where moral hazard exists, we need to beware.

We need to educate and armour our children against betting and we need our government to intervene with protective legislation, curbing the activities of an industry for which creating addictive tendencies in children and adults alike is profitable.

In short

We need to break the taboo and talk to our children, particularly our daughters, about money. We need to teach them the language of money and we need to start young. Research shows their money philosophy is formed before they reach the age of seven. When we improve their financial literacy, we often improve our own. Hand this book over to your children, get them to read this section. Show them the angelic and demonic power of compound returns. Discuss with them, particularly boys, the risks of gambling, the perils of addiction and the manipulative nature of cruel maths.

It could just make a huge difference to their lives.

Chapter Nine

Money, psychology and you
– how to identify and monetise your psychology

We are going to look at money psychology from two perspectives: money and you, and money and the herd. Economists used to create wonderful financial models based on the assumption that investors en masse, in the form of the nebulous, mysterious 'market', always act rationally.

Very often investors both individually and collectively are highly *irrational* – far more driven by emotion than reason. We could cite Einstein's famous maxim here: 'Three great forces rule the world: fear, greed and stupidity.'

Einstein might have been talking about the markets. We shall examine collective hysteria in booms and busts when we look at the psychology of cycles in the next chapter.

But first we need to look at how individual psychology affects investment decisions. How *your* psychology will affect your ability to make money and what to do about it.

Gender comes in here as well. Studies show differences in attitudes towards investments and financial behaviour between genders.

We'll address gender and investment below but first I'd like to pose a question:

Do differences in gender attitudes derive from the original biology of the brain at birth or have they been formed and refined and reinforced by different forms of gender conditioning from early childhood onwards?

A 2019 study published by PNAS, a US scientific research institute, exploring the notion that men have a bigger appetite for risk than women, concluded that such behaviour is learned not inherited.[1] Researchers studied over 500 children from two ethnic groups raised in Yunnan Province, China. Children from the dominant Han community grow up in a traditional patriarchal set-up while the minority Mosuo children are raised in a matrilineal community. Typically, the grandmother heads up the Mosuo household. Women make the decisions while fathers are 'often excluded'. But the groups are educated together at school. Mosuo girls were found to be greater daredevils than Mosuo boys at a younger age but the longer Mosuo children spent with Han students, the more risk-averse the Mosuo girls became, falling behind Mosuo boys by the time they reached eleven. Meanwhile, the Han girls were found to be more risk-averse than Han boys at all ages.

One of the study's co-authors, Elaine M. Liu, associate professor at the University of Houston's Department of Economics, has described the significance of its findings:

> *Many studies find that women are more risk-averse than men. This study tells us that the gender gap in attitudes toward risk among children is influenced by culture and social environment. It may not be an inherited trait. While at the beginning, children's risk-*

taking behaviors follow the norm of their parents, very soon after entering school, their behaviors become more similar to their classmates'. Social environment is important in affecting children's risk attitudes.[2]

This would suggest that how we rear our children, how we inculcate in them attitudes towards risk, and what behaviours they learn in schools, will have a long-lasting influence on their lives in the financial sphere and beyond.

I think it's no coincidence that after a very tomboyish upbringing with my three older brothers and my very active parents – horse-riding, climbing mountains and hurling ourselves into any body of (barely) swimmable water – I developed an attraction to and an aptitude for risk (which on occasion went too far but that's another story). I subsequently went on to a job as an investment banker where my particular speciality was quantifying risk and putting a price on it.

So how do we identify our money psychology?

The first key aspect is to know yourself and to identify your characteristics and how they will affect the investment decisions you are likely to make and whether or not you're better off delegating those decisions to a fund manager.

Are you a procrastinator?

Are you an optimist?

Are you a pessimist?

Do you have a history of smashing remote controls or throwing things other than cricket balls?

Do you suffer from anxiety?

Did your parents inculcate an enjoyment of adventure and risk when you were young?

Do you get to the airport four hours in advance of your flight or do you consider it a huge win if you sprint up to the gate one minute before it closes?

Are you stubborn?

Are you competitive?

How big is your ego?

Can you admit when you're wrong?

Are you an ostrich?

Are you a bear?

Are you a bull?

You get the drift.

Emotional stability

I've mentioned Warren Buffett, the great investment guru. He remarked that, 'You don't need to be a rocket scientist to be a good investor. What you need is emotional stability'.[3] You need an almost Kiplingesque *If* -like sense of phlegmatism, an ability to look upon your financial investments and watch them rise and fall and treat both impostors just the same: no panic selling into a falling market; no fear of missing out buying at the top of the bubble, spurred on by tales of investors awash with profits beyond the dreams of avarice. What you need is:

Psychopathic sang froid

It is no surprise that a disproportionately high percentage of those who work in investment banking are on the sociopathic/psychopathic spectrum.[4]

In a rather cold-blooded way you need to be able both not give a damn while also personally bearing the costs or profits of your own decisions – what the commentator Nassim Nicholas Taleb calls having 'skin in the game'.[5] Quite a few people are capable of not giving much of a damn when they're trading what's known as OPiuM ('Other People's Money'). When I worked on the trading floor at Credit Suisse First Boston, I had an entertaining boss who liked to march up and down the rows of trading desks like a Roman centurion on a trireme exhorting the rowers to pull harder, announcing that we had just lost a house in Clapham or gained a house in Knightsbridge depending on our profit and loss account at the time. It was a useful exercise in reminding us that the numbers with which we played had real meaning. The risk in playing with other people's money is that it distorts investment decisions. We'll come back to that.

The wild sea of investment mistakes

What you also need if you are going to invest your money directly is self-control. A 2018 study from the Sustainable Architecture for Finance in Europe research centre revealed that smokers, a category of people at the lower end of the self-control spectrum, tend to elect to have their money managed by professional advisers because they know this. 'Rather than acting on their own,' the authors explained, 'smokers tie themselves closely to a professional advisor or fund manager and therefore participate in financial markets without taking the risk of jumping into a wild sea of investment mistakes.'[6] As a result (and to the surprise of researchers), smokers' investment portfolios tended to outperform those of non-smokers.

This is a crucial insight. Investor, know thyself.

Gender differences in investing

Different genders tend, on average, to invest differently. These differences lead to professional, or what are deemed 'sophisticated', female investors generally outperforming the same categories of male investors. But, when it comes to the man or woman on the street, the converse is true: men tend to outperform women.

Why is this?

Let's start with professionals and sophisticated investors.

Warwick Business School[7] analysed 2,800 men and women in the UK investing with Barclays Smart Investor over three years. Their results showed that the women outperformed the FTSE 100 Index and outperformed the men.

The women outperformed the FTSE 100 by an annual 1.94 per cent, men by 0.14 per cent.

A separate study by Hargreaves Lansdown[8] reinforced these findings: women outperformed men by an average of 0.81 per cent over a three-year period. The study observed that if this pattern continued for thirty years, the average woman would end up with a portfolio worth 25 per cent more than the average man.

These results were foreshadowed by an earlier study in the US. In 2001, the Massachusetts Institute of Technology published a report called 'Boys will be Boys: Gender, Overconfidence, and Common Stock Investment'.[9] The authors analysed trading activity in over 35,000 households, comparing men and women. They discovered that men trade more frequently than women and do so from a false faith in their own financial acumen. Intriguingly, they discovered that single men traded less sensibly than married men and married men traded less sensibly than single women.

Why do women outperform men in this way?

1   Women take a longer-term view and trade less frequently. The Warwick study observed that while women investors traded on average nine times each year, men traded thirteen times. The Hargreaves Lansdown study found women traded individual shares 49 per cent less frequently than men and traded funds 67 per cent less frequently. There are two issues here. One is trading costs. The more you trade, the more costs you incur and, over time, these costs can erode returns. The second issue is market timing, explored below.

    Boring Money, the UK consumer website (which is anything but), conducted research that showed the average length of time a man held a fund was 8.3 years, compared to 10.7 years for a woman. 'Once invested, women tend to monitor and tweak investments less than men,' says Holly McKay, the founder, adding: 'This has the double whammy of reducing transaction fees, which are a drag on performance, and not trying to time the market, which is almost impossible to do and can backfire.'[10]

2   Women gravitate towards different types of investment, typically less risky and with a more consistent performance history, while men are more likely to invest in riskier investments with potentially higher returns, a form of 'investment thrill-seeking'. The Warwick study revealed how women were more likely to invest in funds rather than the individual stocks favoured by men, thereby diversifying their portfolios and reducing risk and typically leading to fewer losses.

Those women who do invest in the stock market, notably sophisticated investors and/or market professionals, tend to outperform men. However, women as a whole are *less* likely to invest in equities than men.

As we've seen above, one of the reasons that makes women who do invest more likely to outperform men is their greater aversion to risk. But that same female predisposition to avoiding risk can backfire.

Reckless conservatism

Statistics from Her Majesty's Revenue and Customs reveal that women favour cash ISAs over stocks and shares ISAs, with data for the period 2016/17 showing that women were over four and a half times more likely to invest in a cash ISA than a stocks and shares ISA. Men were just under three times as likely.

A YouGov report found that 55 per cent of UK women had never held an equity investment, compared to 37 per cent of men. Only 21 per cent of women said they held a current equity investment, compared to 35 per cent of men.[11]

A global survey by BlackRock Investor Pulse revealed that 72 per cent of women rejected investments in 'riskier' equities, bonds or real estate, compared to 59 per cent of men. The BlackRock data found that 31 per cent of women who had chosen not to invest did so because they feared 'losing everything'. Among men, 27 per cent felt the same way. Similarly, Boring Money found that only 10 per cent of women felt 'very confident' about opening an investment account, compared to 18 per cent of men.

Going broke slowly

Yet, as we've seen, stashing your cash under the mattress will not provide for your old age unless, like the Princess and the Pea, you are perched atop twenty luxury mattresses. Excessive prudence becomes a form of recklessness where the chances of impoverishing yourself in your old age increase rather than decrease.

In short

Discover your investment psychology. Be aware that there is a risk inherent in not taking risks. If you stick all your savings in cash rather than in well-selected stock market investments, you are in danger of going broke slowly as the real value of your savings is eroded over time by inflation. If you recognise that you do not have a money psychology suited to profitably investing in the stock market then don't do it by yourself. Find a financial adviser, pick a good diversified fund where the fund manager makes the decisions for you, or engage in what's known as 'passive investing' – investing in low-cost tracker funds. If you have psychopathic sangfroid and are super-informed financially, then pick a wide range of investments yourself.

Whichever model you choose, invest for the long term. Reinvest your dividends. Sit back and watch your money grow.

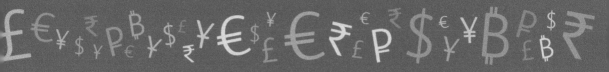

Chapter Ten

Money, psychology and the market

– booms, busts, animal spirits, greater fools and crises: how not to get trampled by the herd and how to bolster your financial resilience

Individual money psychology is one thing but a strange, powerful and often dangerous mentality takes over when herd psychology kicks in. If prices and markets and those who populate the markets were always rational, bubbles and bursts would not exist. But they're not. They're as susceptible to emotion as we are.

And they're not quite as self-aware and omniscient as they might like to think. Professor Frank H. Knight captured this back in the 1920s: 'We perceive the world before we react to it and we react not to what we perceive but to what we infer.'[1] And what we infer can be, and often is, flawed. Market practitioners have a tendency to biased analysis of the world around them. Back in 1957, Professor Hyman Minsky argued that advanced capitalist societies with developed financial institutions are fundamentally unstable and, as a direct result of this bias, are liable to fall into periodic depressions in the aftermath of prolonged periods of euphoria. Minsky's theory has been developed and formalised by Charles Goodhart and Dimitrios Tsomocos in their book *Financial*

Regulation and Stability (2019). Basically, it goes like this: the seeds of bad times are sown in the good. Financial practitioners living through a prolonged good time cannot imagine a bad time and begin to act as if the good times will keep rolling. Winnie the Pooh fans might like to think of it as too many Tiggers and not enough Eeyores. The optimism of the Tiggers[2] distorts their decision-making and they engage in riskier projects. What this means is that when the good times inevitably come to an end, a more severe than otherwise bad time follows because of the increased risk burden created by misplaced optimism.

So, the Tiggers make poor decisions during the good times and then, to compound that, psychological factors make them overreact when the bad times hit. Just like volatile people, the financial world has an inbuilt tendency to overreact. There is a bandwagon effect and a *Torschlusspanik* complex.[3] The bandwagon effect kicks in when people watch an asset class, say gold or tulips or dot-com share prices, start to take off. Keen to participate in the bonanza, more people buy, further pushing up prices and creating a bandwagon effect. The rising prices and the profits made by those already on the bandwagon entice more buyers and so it goes on. At the later stages of a price rise, people will start to become uneasy, feeling that prices have risen way beyond what the asset is actually worth. Yet many of them will still buy on the *greater fool theory:* they rely on being able to sell at some stage in the future to someone who is foolish enough to buy (we saw this with rising US house prices before the 2008 crash). So prices teeter on for a bit, but as they get stratospherically high, more and more people become nervous. Their greed has made them hang on to the asset, but now they finally think: *I want to sell, I want to grab my profits now.* And so they sell, and others see them selling and others see the price begin to dip as more sellers enter the market and then, before you know it, you get *Torschlusspanik!* Everyone is trying to sell into a falling market, pushing down prices even further and faster. And so the bubble bursts.

My favourite bubble is a fragrant one.

Tulip fever

Would you exchange a fine town house in Amsterdam for a tulip bulb? There was a time when many Dutch people were willing to do just that (the Dutch have form here, later going on to exchange a tiny nutmeg-producing island, too small to even feature on a map, for Manhattan).

It all started innocently enough. In seventeenth-century Holland, trading ships began to bring back tulip bulbs from Turkey. The bulbs sprouted into beautiful flowers that became quite the thing in fashionable society. The Dutch began to collect tulip bulbs. And prices began to rise. Suddenly, tulips weren't just a pretty flower, they were a money-making mechanism. As prices rose further, more and more people got in on the act. Fabulous prices began to be achieved by the speculators.

Estimates suggest that, in today's money, the most prized tulip bulbs cost upwards of $750,000. More ordinary bulbs ranged from $50,000 to $150,000. That was beyond the reach of the man and woman on the street, but the ingenious will always find a way to participate in a perceived financial bonanza. Determined to join the party, they devised a scheme whereby they didn't buy an *actual* tulip bulb, but bought *the right to buy* a bulb at the end of the season. This is called a *futures option*. The Dutch described it as *windhandel* ('wind trade') because no actual bulbs changed hands (akin to buying thin air). These buyers never had real money to stump up for the actual tulip bulb, they just wanted to sell their option to another speculator who would pay more for it than they had (the greater fool theory).

Many people made fortunes overnight. Thousands of Dutch cobblers, carpenters, bricklayers and woodcutters jumped on the bandwagon, trading bulb futures in dingy taverns, intoxicated with alcohol and avarice. Some bulbs or futures contracts for bulbs changed hands up to ten times a day. The mania peaked during the winter of 1636–7 when some single bulbs sold for more than ten times the annual income of a skilled craftworker.

Twelve acres of land were offered for a Semper Augustus bulb. By 1637, the price of the Semper had rocketed to 10,000 guilders, enough to feed a family for a lifetime or to buy one of the grandest homes on the most fashionable canal in Amsterdam, complete with a coach house and a large garden.[4]

But then the winds of change began to blow. Outbreaks of bubonic plague kept people from the taverns. Prices had risen so high that most speculators couldn't afford even the cheapest bulbs. This made them throw up their hands and question, for the first time, the viability of the trade. It made them question the sanity of exchanging a gorgeous house for a bulb which looked like an onion. Suddenly the emperor had no clothes. Prices plummeted. Then in February 1637 the bubble burst.

In the twentieth and twenty-first centuries, commentators used the term *bubble* to describe Japan's asset price inflation, the speculative dot-com rise and fall, and the sub-prime crisis.

Back in November 2013, former president of De Nederlandsche Bank (the central bank of the Netherlands), Nout Wellink, described

You paid WHAT?

the speculation around bitcoin as 'worse than tulip mania. At least then you got a tulip, now you get nothing.' Not quite true, as the earlier section on bitcoin has shown. It does have value, but there is no doubt that prices have been driven high by speculators. Will they rise further? Only time will tell …

Why do bubbles happen?

We discussed bandwagons and *Torschlusspanik* earlier. Let's take a look at *animal spirits*.

It's fashionable in economics to regard markets as just a bunch of numbers. The underlying assumption is that if you are good at numbers you'll be good at the markets. This belief has reached its apotheosis in high-frequency trading via computers. Acting on complex algorithms, these computers trade at terrifyingly high frequencies in staggeringly huge amounts. Based on the data fed into them and the algorithms that program their behaviour, they make their own decisions at superfast speeds without any further human input (see the earlier section on high-frequency trading in Chapter Seven).

When humans actively make decisions they are mainly based on data. But here's the thing. There beats in the market, hidden beneath the patina of numbers, a wild and savage heart. And hidden in the streams of numbers that pass through the market like electronic blood, there breathes an animal spirit.[5]

A lot of commentators and academics don't like to admit this. They would like the market to conform to rational scientific examination. Sometimes it does. Until it doesn't. Until it appears to go mad.

Because here's the thing about markets. Models are necessary but not sufficient. Numbers and machines play a huge role. But so do humans. And we humans are not always rational or predictable. We are susceptible to emotions and crowds of humans will behave differently to the individuals who make up those crowds. When a panic ensues, for most, all sophistication flies out of the window and fear and desperation take over.

The emotional life cycle of a bubble

- ▶ Excitement: something new comes along and piques our interest.

- ▶ Love: we think it's the best thing ever and commit wholeheartedly to it.

- ▶ Greed: we can't get enough of it.

- ▶ Disillusionment: suddenly we're not so sure.

- ▶ Panic: we've got to get out of here. NOW!

- ▶ Divorce: we do, and boy does it cost us.

Or:

- ▶ Flavour of the month

- ▶ Bandwagon

- ▶ FOMO ('fear of missing out')

- ▶ *Torschlusspanik*

- ▶ Crash

The **ULTIMATE** INVESTMENT ALGORITHM

After hundreds of hours of intense thought ...

After several more hundreds of hours of intense thought ...

The **ULTIMATE** INVESTMENT ALGORITHM by Prof. A. Smithers

$$\frac{42 - x(y)}{z} *$$

* where
$x = stupidity$
$y = greed$
$z = fear$

Now we are entering the fascinating realm of behavioural economics, a relatively new discipline which attempts to incorporate insights into human psychology into the realm of economics. In 2017, the father of the movement, Richard Thaler, was awarded the Nobel Prize.

The biggest recent example of the market not behaving as all the models would suggest was during the sub-prime meltdown of 2008 and 2009.

The 2007–10 global financial crisis: legislative liberalisation, fear, greed and stupidity

'It is well enough that people of the nation do not understand our banking and monetary system, for if they did, I believe there would be a revolution before tomorrow morning,' said Henry Ford (founder of the eponymous car empire) over a hundred years ago.[6]

Ford had, and has, a point. This crisis was incubated by politicians, fuelled by moral hazard, built upon a giant financial sleight of hand, and facilitated by wilful ignorance. It impoverished many, enriched a few, and the aftershocks are still being felt. It was the biggest financial disaster since the Great Depression (until coronavirus came along). It originated in the United States, but as a result of globalisation and the interconnectedness of the world's economies, it threatened the financial system of the entire world. The financial system began to haemorrhage so much money that for a while it threatened to collapse. In the end, taxpayers rescued it. You and I rescued it. To the tune of $2.8 trillion.[7]

How it started

In 1999, Bill Clinton decided to loosen the regulatory controls designed to curb the excesses of the financial system. One of the ways in which he did this was by abolishing the Glass–Steagall Act.

As part of wider provisions contained within the 1933 Banking Act, Glass–Steagall was enacted by the US Government as a response to the Great Depression. It was designed to separate the activities of investment banks and commercial banks, specifically to protect the deposits of the person on the street from the risky adventuring of investment bankers. Glass–Steagall did its job pretty well. Until Clinton abolished it.

As a result of the repeal of Glass–Steagall and inflows of cash as foreigners bought up increasing amounts of US dollar securities, investment bankers were fuelled with access to LOTS of extra cash whilst simultaneously being given access once again to the person on the street. They made ample use of both and grew ever richer. The person on the street seemed to benefit too, at least for a while. Many people who had previously been deemed 'untouchable' found that mortgage lenders were hurling money at them. This was also a result of another political decision made in the mid 1990s by Bill Clinton, who instructed government-sponsored mortgage lenders Fannie Mae and Freddie Mac to lend to these people.

Clinton's successor, George Bush, pursued the liberalising, mortgage-pushing, home-owning agenda with a zeal of his own. Vowing to 'use the mighty muscle of the federal government' to bring a target of over five million new homeowners into being, he insisted that Fannie Mae and Freddie Mac meet ambitious new goals for low-income lending and persuaded Congress to spend as much as $200 million a year to help first-time buyers with down payments and purchase costs, even when they had saved not a single dime themselves.

Home ownership for the many was a beautiful dream spun by Clinton and Bush alike.

You could say this was a humanitarian act, or you might see it as a political ploy to garner votes. One thing is certain: it was not a decision based on sound economics.

The crucible of the global financial crisis was something called 'sub-prime'. Sub-prime was basically lending to people who had hitherto been deemed too high risk to borrow money. Effectively financial untouchables. *Prime* suggests tip-top, *sub*-prime implies something just a level below tip-top, but in reality these unfortunate people were anything but prime. They were a MASSIVE RISK. In some cases, they had No Income, No Job and No Down payments. The financial community, with its love of acronyms, named these NINJA loans.

Predatory lending

Here's one such. In Bakersfield, California, a Mexican strawberry picker earning $14,000 a year was lent every last cent he needed to buy a house for $724,000. (OK, he did have some income, but not enough to service that monumental debt for long.)

Welcome to the world of predatory lending: lending to people who are never going to be able to repay.

You might ask, why on earth would anyone lend money to people who are highly unlikely to pay it back, ever? Why would anyone want to be a predatory lender?

The answer is that no one with skin in the game would. But the mortgage brokers who sold these loans participated in a phenomenon which meant that they did NOT have skin in the game, which meant they did not suffer when the loans went bad. But they did gain, earning a commission on every mortgage they sold.

How was this possible?

Financial alchemy

It was possible thanks to an innovation created by investment banks. They, in all their brilliance, bought these mortgages, packaged them up into financial instruments called enhanced mortgage-backed securities, and sold them on. In dizzying numbers.[8] Between 2003 and 2011, $5,169 billion mortgage-backed securities were issued in the United States (see the section on money and scale in 'Money miscellany' to conceptualise these figures). The investment banks then sold these on to insurance companies and pension funds, having magically transmogrified the apparent risk profile of these investments to make them look acceptable to these supposedly conservative institutions. They turned these financial instruments into an unlikely and contradictory pairing of high return and low risk. The ratings agencies classified these instruments as low risk because they were geographically diverse and had been spliced and diced into different layers of risk. The best bets – the slices at the top – were those being offered as 'enhanced'. The worst were at the bottom. The reality was the enhanced ones were better than the worst bets, but they were still never a good or a safe bet. But the relativity and the rating did the trick in a dazzling financial sleight of hand, born of ignorance at best and money-grubbing at worst. The ratings agencies got paid by the originators of the bonds to be rated. Now that's a lovely conflict of interest, isn't it? Moral hazard strikes again.

This financial sleight of hand was VERY successful.

Moral hazard

This whole tower was built on a series of conflicts of interest, starting with the mortgage broker. The broker was highly incentivised to sell loans without having ANY incentive to make sure they would be repaid. The securitisation and sale of these loans divorced the lending of money from the repercussions of failure, breaking one of the most fundamental tenets of banking integrity: only lend to people who can pay you back. It also institutionalised moral hazard.[9]

You might say that it was great that these people were given money to buy their own homes. And, in some ways, you'd be right, but most of them paid a terrible price. There were two nasty stings in the tail of most of these sub-prime loans. First of all, the loans were not on fixed interest rates but variable. They started off with 'teaser' levels of interest, enticingly low. But well-hidden in the small print was the first sting. Typically after two years, the interest rate ratcheted up, increasing mortgage payments dramatically, imperilling the borrowers' ability to service their loans.

The second sting came because the value of the mortgage equalled (or in some cases even exceeded) the value of the house. This meant that if house prices fell even a little then technically the home owner would be bankrupt as they would owe more than their asset was worth. In theory, they could live with that, so long as they could continue to pay the monthly mortgage interest payments and didn't have to sell their property and repay the mortgage.

Going broke fast

What happened was horrible. When the teaser levels fell away and the interest rates kicked up, the borrowers could no longer service their mortgages and they fell into default. They went bankrupt. Nearly *ten million* homeowners lost their homes to foreclosure sales in the US between 2006 and 2014.

As the American dream died and house prices began to tumble,[10] the financial markets finally started to realise that, with regard to sub-prime mortgages, the emperor really did have no clothes. Predictably, they began to panic. The panic led to the mass selling of bundles of sub-prime assets which had been turned into financial instruments that allowed them to be sold on around the world. This panic became a contagion across asset classes, with the prices of what really *were* prime assets falling as institutions desperately tried to sell the only thing other institutions were actually willing to buy (a so-called *flight to quality*), leading to a dramatic shortage of cash in the markets. Leading to the bankruptcy and failure of some of the largest financial institutions in the world and widespread bailouts of those which were on the brink of failing.

Why, as the Queen asked when she visited the London School of Economics a few years later, did nobody see it coming?

Well, a few brave and brilliant investors did and they devised ways of shorting[11] the sub-prime instruments (essentially, placing bets that their value was going to fall). But the overwhelming majority of observers and practitioners did not see it coming. The financial models of the economists and the most sophisticated financiers did not see it coming. The machines did not see it coming. Governments did not see it coming. They were all looking the wrong way. They were expecting a completely different crisis, potentially arising from the huge Chinese holdings of US government debt and what might happen if the Chinese sold it off. That was, and remains, a fair worry. But it didn't happen back then.

So why do crashes and crises so often seem to take everyone by surprise?

Bandwagons and bursting bubbles are by no means the only reasons why markets crash. Volcanic eruptions, extreme weather, wars, famines and plagues have devastated communities, nations and economies since time immemorial. Just as coronavirus is doing now.

Black swans – the realm of the unknown

Every so often, something completely out of the blue comes along. Floored, we shake our heads in amazement. We never saw it coming. Why not? Because our experience so far did not tell us to factor in such a possibility. If all we've ever seen all our lives are white swans then, when a black one comes along, we are amazed and mystified.[12] We didn't know they existed. Also, more subtly, we weren't aware that we didn't know they existed. This might sound like gobbledygook but isn't. The quotation below comes from Donald Rumsfeld, the then US Secretary of Defence, speaking in 2002 on the subject of US military policy in Iraq:

> As we know, there are known knowns. There are things we know we know. We also know there are known unknowns. That is to say we know there are some things

we do not know. But there are also unknown unknowns,
the ones we don't know we don't know.

This isn't doublespeak. This is brilliant. For it is the things that we don't know we don't know that come hurtling out of the blue and slap us in the face. These things can be bad but they can also be good and we need to be ready to deal with both. The banker in the illustration opposite knows he is navigating a mine field (of, let's say, toxic debts) but what he doesn't know is that the spectre of a pandemic is creeping up on him.

My favourite example of a black swan event is given in the book of that name by the man who invented the term: the brilliant contrarian thinker Nassim Nicholas Taleb.

He describes 365 days in the life of an American turkey.

Day 1: The turkey wakes up in his nice secure turkey house. Some friendly human comes trundling along, lets him out to roam in a nice safe yard, gives him fresh food and clean water then, when night falls, the human shuts him back in his nice, cosy, safe turkey house.

Day 2 – Day 363: Same as above.

Day 364: The nice kind human comes along with a meat cleaver and chops off his head.

Day 365: He is cooked and eaten for Thanksgiving.

Now, the turkey just didn't see it coming. Nothing in his prior experience had led him to think that his pet human would come along, decapitate and eat him. But the human did. And the lesson is this: we cannot reliably use the past as an unfailingly accurate predictor of the future. We can use it but we cannot rely solely on our experience of the past. We have to add in other factors, the unknown unknowns, to protect ourselves from s**t happening in life – and in the world of finance too.

But how can you prepare for things that you don't know you don't know? The answer lies in creativity. *Think, imagine.* Let me share another of my favourite quotations, this time from George Bernard Shaw: 'You think of things that are and ask why. I dream of things that never were and ask why not?'[13]

Coronavirus

Coronavirus is a black swan event. The tragic death toll of this virus, our fears of it, the containment efforts implemented, have all had a dramatic effect on the economy, on financial markets, on our personal finances and on mental health, substance abuse, domestic violence and gambling to name a few of the other devastating consequences. Epidemiologists among others have long-predicted the coming of a pandemic. Their attitude was not *if* but *when*. No one can predict the when, so it's fair to say we were all taken by surprise.

In the UK, economists are predicting an annual fall in gross domestic product, a measure of economic output, of 10 per cent, possibly as much as 15 per cent. Stock markets have fallen hard and fast. Since its peak of 7,877 in May 2019, the UK FTSE 100 (the index of the one hundred largest companies quoted on the London Stock Exchange) has fallen by over 36 per cent and in late March 2020 was hovering around 5,000. In the United States, the initial 20 per cent fall in the S&P 500[14] from its 19 February high took just sixteen days. This was the fastest ever such fall. As of 18 March 2020, it had fallen a whopping 30 per cent.

Markets have been driven down by rational decision-making but also by panic and by *Torschlusspanik*: wanting to sell before others do. A *get out while you can* mentality. Falling markets develop a momentum of their own. Algorithmic, machine-based trading and the growing share of the market occupied by tracker funds (which develop an inbuilt market-destabilizing bias as a result of their proliferation and internal functioning) have also driven down the market. This is why we have seen some of the most dramatic daily stock price percentage falls in the lifetimes of many practitioners. We are likely to see sharp fluctuations as markets spike up and then down again as good news and bad news waxes and wanes.

Some commentators believe that the markets, rather than overreacting due to fear, are *under-reacting*, based on excessive optimism. It's also possible that other factors we haven't yet managed to unearth are keeping the markets unreasonably high. Perhaps it is the quantitative easing that governments around the globe have undertaken to try to bolster their economies. Perhaps it is due to fears of inflation, though many commentators fear deflation. Sitting in the middle of a crisis, the truth is, *no one really knows*. They might think they do, but all we have now is opinions. We are all operating in the realm of the unknown.

So how could/should we have prepared for this and other unanticipated black swan events?

The point is, although we don't know the exact nature of the crises on the horizon, we do know that, sooner or later, they will come. This knowledge helps us plan.

'Plans are worthless, but planning is everything', said Dwight Eisenhower, who before his stint as president of the United States was supreme commander of the Allied Expeditionary Force in Europe during the Second World War. It's fair to say that Eisenhower knew a thing or two about planning. He argued that the details of a plan which was designed years in advance would often turn out to be incorrect, but that the planning process demanded the exploration of options and contingencies which in turn forces us to ask crucial questions.

History has shown that we almost inevitably plan for the wrong crisis. Because we can rarely foresee the right crisis, we need to armour ourselves against crises in general by putting in place financial contingencies.

Preparing for crises: financial resilience

This is a huge topic and I'm going to stick to the broader philosophy of financial planning or we'll all still be here in a year's time wading through the details.

If humanly possible, we should try to live within our means so that we have a monthly buffer between our income and our outgoings as well as savings that hold their value. In a crash, the only thing that almost invariably holds its value is cash. We've seen how over the long term inflation can erode the value of cash (and, in countries plagued by hyperinflation, in the short term too, as we saw in Chapter Six) and I encourage you not to hold too much of your assets in cash should that high-order problem be applicable to you. However, we always need to keep a cash buffer whether it's in physical cash or bank deposits. In an ideal world, cash reserves equivalent to six months of outgoings would be prudent, although I fully realise that for many people this is not possible. (The understandable refusal of many retailers to accept physical cash during the pandemic has underscored the need for bank deposits though in other, non-pandemic crises, physical cash is likely to be more useful.) Holding reserves of cash or bank deposits can see us through sudden, unexpected falls in our income or increases in prices. Gold also tends to hold its value although interestingly when the coronavirus sell-off first hit, gold prices fell because holders of gold ended up selling the only thing that people really wanted to buy – gold – although the price has rebounded since.

The other thing about having a buffer of cash or cash equivalents in these situations is that it can offer what some money managers have called 'the buying opportunity of a generation'. If you believe that economies and markets will recover then market sell-offs such as occasioned by coronavirus provide unique opportunities to buy into the market. If you have a long-term perspective then having this inbuilt financial resilience can create a virtuous circle that further bolsters your financial health.

In short

That amorphous thing we call 'the market' can and does, just like the rest of us, have meltdowns. The market, again just like the rest of us – because it is, essentially, *us* – is susceptible to the psychological spectrum that produces bubbles and their inevitable aftermath, crashes. Think of the crashes as the mother of all hangovers when the party's gone on way too long. We could have tried to see what was coming, we could have left the party early, but few of us do. When you see the markets partying, be cautious. It might not be the time to keep buying. It might just be the time to sell.

It helps to be contrarian. To not think like the herd. To not act like the herd. But to anticipate what the herd will do and take pre-emptive action. Sell before they do. Sometimes the markets can drop precipitously because of events such as coronavirus, but often they fall beyond a rational level, driven lower by fear. Sometimes, seemingly illogically, they don't fall as far as economic predictions might appear to warrant. Without wishing to sound too Cassandra-like, sooner or later something bad *will* happen. If you can possibly avoid doing so, those times are not the times to sell. You risk getting mown down in *Torschlusspanik* as everyone panics and runs for the door. They could just be the times to buy if you have cash or cash equivalents like bank deposits. Endeavour, if humanly possible, to live within your means so that you can amass the cash and bank deposits which will serve as a buffer when the bad times hit. Search the blue skies for the black swans that will hurtle out of nowhere and break your arm. And your bank.

Understanding the psychology of the market might just help you to avoid the worst effects of the crashes that have plagued the world throughout financial history.

And, finally, when you are engaging in any kind of transaction, beware moral hazard.

Money miscellany

The money world is too fascinating to stop here. Time for a few digressions before I go.

1. Money and scale

It's easy to become blinded by the number of zeros that follow the measures we use to describe the 'moneyverse'. We might know that there are twelve zeros in a trillion; that a trillion is a thousand billion; that a billion is a thousand million. But like chickens who supposedly count *one, two, three* then have to leap to *many* chickens as the numbers grow too big to fathom, how on earth can we conceptualise these huge sums? One useful way is to convert money sums into time.

For instance:

1 million seconds equates to twelve days

1 billion seconds equates to thirty-two years

1 trillion seconds amounts to over 31,709 years and would take us back to the era of sabre-toothed tigers

2. Money and barter

Many (by no means all) economic theories maintain that money evolved from barter. They posit that once money had evolved, barter had no real role to play. But swapping assets always has and always will have a role to play and can bypass money and not just when a currency is dying due to issues like hyperinflation.

My favourite trade in the entire history of barter was an exchange of land, perhaps the greatest property deal of all time. Money very much did exist at this time but barter is so useful that money can sometimes be sidelined.

It happened on 31 July 1667. All because of *Myristica fragrans*, the spice known as nutmeg. The Dutch were obsessed by nutmeg. Not only did it make their food taste nice but it was also believed to provoke hallucinations (nutmeg benders) and to be an aphrodisiac. (Though nutmeg has its dark side: it's poisonous to various animals, including dogs, and taken by humans in excess can cause palpitations, nausea and pain.) The pod-like nutmeg seeds were worn for protection by the few who could afford them during the bubonic plague. This might sound like an old wives' tale but the nutmeg might have deterred the fleas that carried the disease, sparing the wearer a fatal bite.

Lots of people were obsessed by nutmeg. Wars were fought over it as if it were an edible Helen of Troy. Often the markup between what nutmeg was sold for when it left the Indonesian islands where it was grown, to what it was sold for when it reached the dinner tables of the rich, was 6,000 per cent. Nutmeg had always been expensive. A fourteenth-century German price table reveals that a pound of it cost as much as 'seven fat oxen'.

But the Dutch got greedy. They wanted to corner the market, control supply and force the price still higher.

The Dutch were close to cornering the market but not close enough. They owned a tantalising nine of the ten Banda Islands in Indonesia: home to all the world's nutmeg trees. To make matters worse, the tenth Island, called Run, was owned by their arch-enemy, the British. So the Dutch proposed a trade. They would give the British a small, swampy spit of land called New Amsterdam in return for a tiny volcanic island so small it does not even register on most maps of Indonesia. The British agreed.

The Dutch thought they had done very well.

So did the British.

The Dutch got Run.

The Brits got Manhattan.

3. Money and ecological economics; an alternative look at compound interest; the distinction between wealth and money; Soddy's ball of gold

Frederick Soddy was a brilliant chemist who won the 1921 Nobel Prize in Chemistry. He also turned his talents to economics, which he believed lacked a connection to biophysical reality. His 1926 book *Wealth, Virtual Wealth and Debt: The Solution of the Economic Paradox* is viewed today as a key inspiration to the study of ecological economics. Soddy drew an interesting distinction between wealth and finance. He wrote that real wealth, like life itself, depends on energy and is subject to the laws of thermodynamics, rotting, rusting or degrading with age, while money and debt (virtual wealth) constitute accounting devices invented by humans and are subject only to the laws of mathematics. Rather than decaying, virtual wealth, in the form of debt or credit compounding at an annual rate of interest, grows without bounds. He did not consider this a good thing.

He illustrated this distinction with his 'ball of gold' calculation.

Soddy hypothesized that if you owned a nine-inch ball of gold, converted it to money, lent it out at 5 per cent per annum, sat back idly for 1,070 years, then converted the money back into gold, you would end up with a golden ball the size of the earth, weighing four times as much. He decried this conversion of perishable wealth into everlasting loans to derive a permanent future income as a kind of deadly alchemy, calling it the obsession of his era. He saw this as confusion over the real nature of wealth and invited readers to contemplate an era where people lived off the interest of their mutual indebtedness: a financial equivalent of everybody taking in everybody else's dirty laundry.

Food for thought and a modern twist on Aristotle's barren money theory (see below).

4. Money and morality

Money has long been freighted with morality rather than being seen as neutral. The Bible has it that love of money is the root of all evil. Equally, George Bernard Shaw's adage that it is *the lack of money* that is the root of all evil also carries weight.

Borrowing and lending money bear the heaviest historical baggage. Aristotle condemned the lending of money in ancient Greece, describing money as 'barren':

> The most hated sort [of moneymaking], and with the greatest reason, is usury, which makes a gain out of money itself, and not from the natural use of it. For money was intended to be used in exchange, but not to increase at interest. And this term usury, which means the birth of money from money, is applied to the breeding of money, because the offspring resembles the parent. Wherefore of all modes of making money this is the most unnatural.

In fourteenth-century Italy, the poet Dante consigned usurers to the seventh circle of Hell, weighed down till eternity by their greed.

Shylock the money lender in *The Merchant of Venice* is a notorious figure of hate. Opposition to Jewish usurers was often violent. In 1190, the Jews of York were massacred by agents of the nobility, who owed money to the Jews that they did not wish to repay.

Pogroms against Jews, which involved the burning of financial records as well as the murder of the moneylenders themselves, were commonplace in many parts of Europe. Hatred of moneylenders is as ancient as money itself. And while excessive rates of interest such as those charged by modern payday lenders are a major issue, where would we be without the ability to borrow money? Those who lend us money facilitate a kind of time travel of assets from future dreams to present reality. How else would most of us ever buy a home without borrowing money?

5. Money and shame

When we look at phenomena like the sub-prime crisis and the huge sums of money made by practitioners, many of whom were subsequently bailed out by us, the taxpayers, we might ask ourselves what happened to the concept of shame. Although a troubling concept psycho-therapeutically, it has in the past acted as a useful brake on, among other things, financial malpractice. But shame is employed today as a powerful tool. Time to travel to Spain to meet the *cobrador del frac*. This frock-coated, top-hatted, briefcase-carrying debt-collector is employed by banks and other creditors to stand outside an office, a house, or beside someone's table in a restaurant, conveying to the world that this particular person has not paid their debts. Naming and shaming them.

'The figure of the *cobrador* is so well known he doesn't have to say anything', says Juan Lorca, manager of the Barcelona office of the Cobrador del Frac, a company with branches all over Spain and Portugal and which has been chasing debtors for the past twenty-five years.

All they have to do is stand there. They never speak to the subject. They never do more than hand the debtor our card. Even for the most shameless people there will be some situation where they don't want the *cobrador* to appear. So we send him where it will do the most harm, usually his place of work, especially on the day when his suppliers or clients or financiers are visiting him. This usually encourages him to pay up.

6. Money and the supernatural

We have an interesting relationship with money where, on the one hand, we see it as an everyday object, and, on the other, we imbue it with supernatural power. We can see this in two distinct ways:

i. Appeasing and paying the spirits

The ancient Greeks used to put silver coins called obols into the mouths of dead people so that they might pay the ferryman, Charon, to transport their body across the River Styx to Hades. For centuries, Chinese mourners have burnt joss paper, known as 'ghost money', at the graves of their ancestors in the hope of bestowing upon them a happy and prosperous afterlife. Also in China, coins bearing images of swords are hung above the beds of the sick to ward off evil spirits. In Germany, silver medals were thought to offer protection from the plague. And from the time of the first Crusades back in the eleventh century, English knights wore silver coin charms to invoke the protection of St George, the patron saint of horsemen.

ii. Seeking supernatural inspiration

Intriguingly, what many might regard as supernatural forces have been harnessed in an attempt to make money on the stock market. It's a closely guarded secret on Wall Street and in other financial centres that some of the seemingly most hard-nosed practitioners consult astrologers. One of the best known astrological investors is Arch Crawford. Crawford started his career as a trader and technical analyst at Merrill Lynch in the early 1960s before discovering astrology. He's been publishing his forecasts, which mingle technical analysis with astrological input, since 1977. Crawford made one of his most dramatic and memorable predictions in 1987, in his 8 August newsletter, where he warned of an imminent, horrendous stock market crash. He advised his readers to 'be out of all stocks by August 24',[1] revealing that unusual 'geocentric planetary arrangements' would end the bull run in stock markets.

His prediction was met with widespread scepticism, ridicule and amusement. The prevailing view was that hardly anyone can call the top of a bull market, let alone by reading the stars. The market seemed to be powering along with an unstoppable momentum, thank you very much.

But on 25 August something interesting happened: the Dow Jones Industrial Average hit 2,722 points, a whopping 73 per cent higher than its level of 1,570 on 31 January 1986 and the peak of a bull market that had stampeded on for close to five years.

And then ... it began to head downwards, drifting at first, until, on 19 October, 'Black Monday', the Dow fell off a cliff, plummeting 508 points and losing 22.6 per cent of its total value – the largest ever one-day percentage fall in its history. Crawford's pinpoint prediction was uncannily accurate and rarer than a black swan. When asked how he did this, Crawford answered:

> Basically I spent a lot of time setting up and projecting conventional cycles and trends. These would develop naturally if nothing interrupted them. I then look for forthcoming planetary configurations which might disrupt them in some way, and make my calls according to how I understand what the disruption most probably will be.

Astrological consultation is not a new thing.

Back in the nineteenth century, the legendary financier J. P. Morgan also consulted an astrologer, Evangeline Adams. Morgan commented that while mere millionaires may not need to consult an astrologer, billionaires do.

And finally …

7. The five stages of an investment banking deal

The dynamic shown opposite is one that was well familiar to me during my investment banking years.

Euphoria

Despair

The hunt for the guilty

The punishment of the innocent

The rewarding of the uninvolved

It might sound in parts as if I'm anti the financial services sector, but the truth is I'm not. I just believe we need to focus on what it is, what it does and how it does it, and be ready to intervene to curb its excesses before any wildfires ignite into an unstoppable inferno.[2] Let it be noted that, in 2018, the financial services sector contributed £132 billion to the UK economy, 6.9 per cent of its total economic output, and paid £29 billion in tax. It employed 1.1 million people, 3.1 per cent of the total employed in the UK.[3] In 2018, finance and insurance represented 7.4 per cent (or $1.5

trillion) of US gross domestic product and employed more than 6.3 million people.

That pays for a lot of schools, teachers, hospitals, doctors, nurses, police and firefighters.

The financial services sector also gave me my first proper job and it was a lot more congenial and better paid than waitressing in a rugby club, being a sales assistant in Etam or sanding down cars, which were my previous three jobs. It put me into the heart of the money world, taught me how it works, showed me when it doesn't, gave me insights I would never have gleaned from the outside. It bought me freedom to write. It inspired my first novel, *Nest of Vipers*, which went on to become a global bestseller. It taught me how to understand and speak the language of money, which I hope to have shared with you here.

Postscript

Money is one of the most important languages on the planet. If we can understand and speak it better we can improve our financial health, our physical health and our mental health.

I hope that *10 Things* will help us arm ourselves against the slippery and sometimes fragile nature of fiat money; protect against fraud, hacking and the disruption of being locked out of our bank accounts by technological meltdowns; harness the power of financial angels and avoid the demons; teach our children about money, boosting their and our own financial literacy; learn to recognise our own money psychology and how to monetise it; appreciate how sometimes not taking risks is riskier than taking them; discover where to put our money to keep it safe, and where not to; learn that financial markets have emotions and behave irrationally, just like us; see how there is a bias towards optimism that veils dangers; and discover how to dodge the worst effects of crises and crashes.

In short, I hope it will help us strengthen our financial resilience and health.

But not just ours.

In the investment section, I refer to **environmental, social and governance** considerations (ESG) and the **third bottom line**. This is the concept where we judge companies not just by the *profits* they make but by their impact on *people* and on the *planet*.

It seems like now might be a particularly good time to start applying it.

As I write this, during the coronavirus lockdown in March 2020, some companies are distinguishing themselves by taking measures to protect and bolster the welfare of their employees and customers. Others are not. We shall remember this and many of us will vote with our wallets to reward or punish these companies accordingly. But there's also another way in which we can bring our voice to bear on different companies and influence the way they do business.

We can buy shares in them.

Buying shares in listed companies gives us a voice. We can use this voice at annual general meetings. We don't have to be huge pension funds making investments of hundreds of millions of pounds. Just buying as little as one share will get us an invitation to the annual general meeting and an opportunity to raise our hands and voice our concerns and wishes to the company's management. This is financial democracy in action. For some but not all classes of shares (there are ALWAYS caveats and exceptions in the financial world), it is one share, one vote. Money talks. But you don't always need to have a ton of it to be heard.

We can attempt to influence the direction a company takes through our collective voice as minority shareholders if we band together with other small shareholders and we leverage our influence via social media and traditional media, which always like a good David versus Goliath story. We can vote with our cash and invest in the businesses which will deliver the greatest return – for profit, for people and for the planet. There are ratings agencies which measure companies' commitment to ESG and the third bottom line. They can help us to identify companies to invest in, companies which could do better and companies to shun. If we find ourselves invested in a company who could do better on the ESG front, we can encourage them to improve. Or we can deliberately invest a small amount in them to gain access to their annual meetings where we can use our voice. I'm not talking witch-hunts: I'm talking judicious use of message magnification.

This is nudge theory at work. Small, incremental movements can effect sizeable change. We just have to start them, first by ourselves, then by grouping together and magnifying our voice.

Understanding the language of money and putting that knowledge to work gives us a voice we can use to this end. I believe it is better to use that voice from within rather than shouting inaudibly from the wrong side of the window.

Fluency in the language of money can impact much more than just our own financial health. Profit, people, planet. That is something worth shouting about.

Useful resources

The Money Advice Service is an impartial body, funded by the Department for Work and Pensions, tasked with helping people to make the most out of their money and pensions. They offer detailed advice on how to save money, types of savings, how to invest money, and different types of investment.

The Money Charity and Martin Lewis's **MoneySavingExpert.com** provide two other useful sources of advice and information.

When checking out the credentials of financial advisers, two helpful websites are **VouchedFor** and **Unbiased**, while further unbiased advice can be sought from **Citizens Advice**.

Boring Money is another brilliant and informative website (and not at all boring) that offers independent advice and is completely transparent about how it makes money (thereby avoiding moral hazard and potential bias in its recommendations). The website's founder, Holly Mackay, makes this promise:

> *We are talking to you about your money. Any investment firm we say we like, we like. And we would say that to our sisters, our friends, our kids' teachers ... We don't just say nice things about people who pay us the most.*

As well as not being spivvy, this makes commercial sense. If you lot trust us, you'll read our stuff and we'll be relevant. If you don't trust us, you won't visit the site and we'll just disappear.

Another excellent online resource is **This is Money**, which is aimed at supporting non-professionals to be their own financial adviser. There are also various online publications which can be helpful in familiarising you with the investing world and what to look for – **trustnet.com**, **morningstar.co.uk** and **ii.co.uk** are just a few of the many resources out there – while for those wishing to choose their own investments, **Barclays Smart Investor** offers a variety of services.

The Financial Conduct Authority, the conduct regulator for the financial sector in the UK, can help with any issues of potential malpractice.

Debtors Anonymous is a twelve-step programme for people who want to get their borrowing under control.

Gambling with Lives (the latter a charity founded by Charles and Liz Ritchie after their son Jack killed himself at the age of 24 while addicted to gambling) provides help and support to those who need it.

Further reading

Aliber, Robert Z., and Charles P. Kindleberger, *Manias, Panics, and Crashes: A History of Financial Crises* (7th edn, London: Palgrave Macmillan, 2015)

Antonopoulos, Andreas M., *The Internet of Money: A Collection of Talks* (Scotts Valley: CreateSpace, 2016)

Antonopoulos, Andreas M., *The Internet of Money: Volume Three: A Collection of Talks* (London: Book Depository, 2019)

Antonopoulos, Andreas M., *The Internet of Money: Volume Two: A Collection of Talks* (London: Book Depository, 2017)

Ariely, Dan, *Predictably Irrational: The Hidden Forces that Shape our Decisions* (rev. edn, London: Harper, 2009)

Atwood, Margaret, *Payback: Debt and the Shadow Side of Wealth* (London: Bloomsbury, 2009)

Augar, Philip, *The Bank that Lived a Little: Barclays in the Age of the Very Free Market* (London: Penguin, 2019)

Boden, Anne, *The Money Revolution: Easy Ways to Manage Your Finances in a Digital World* (London: Kogan Page, 2019)

Clancy, Kevin, *A History of the Sovereign: Chief Coin of the World* (Llantrisant: Royal Mint, 2015)

Cohan, William D., *House of Cards: How Wall Street's Gamblers Broke Capitalism* (London: Penguin, 2009)

Davies, Glyn, *A History of Money* (4th edn, Cardiff: University of Wales Press, 2016) – yes, he is my father!

Ferguson, Niall, *The Ascent of Money: A Financial History of the World* (London: Penguin, 2019)

Ferguson, Niall, *The House of Rothschild: Money's Prophets 1798–1848* (London: Penguin, 1999)

Ferguson, Niall, *The House of Rothschild: The World's Banker 1849–1999* (rev. edn, London: Penguin, 2000)

Geithner, Timothy F., *Stress Test: Reflections on Financial Crises* (New York: Crown Publishing, 2014)

Goodheart, Charles, and Dimitrios P. Tsomocos, *Financial Regulation and Stability: Lessons from the Global Financial Crisis* (Cheltenham: Edward Elgar Publishing, 2019)

Gregory, Deborah W., *Unmasking Financial Psychopaths: Inside the Minds of Investors in the Twenty-First Century* (London: Palgrave Macmillan, 2014)

Hockenhull, Thomas (ed.), *Symbols of Power: Ten Coins that Changed the World* (London: British Museum Press, 2015)

Kenvyn, Abigail, *Inside the Royal Mint: An Introduction to the Royal Mint Experience* (Llantrisant: Royal Mint, 2016)

King, Mervyn, *The End of Alchemy: Money, Banking and the Future of the Global Economy* (London: Abacus, 2017)

Knight, Frank H., *Risk, Uncertainty and Profit* (Boston, MA: Houghton Mifflin Company, 1921)

Levitt, Steven D., and Stephen J. Dubner, *Freakonomics: A Rogue Economist Explores the Hidden Side of Everything* (London: Penguin, 2007)

Lewis, Michael, *The Big Short: Inside the Doomsday Machine* (London: Penguin, 2011) – Lewis's other books are also highly recommended

Martin, Felix, *Money: The Unauthorised Biography* (London: Vintage, 2014)

McDonald, Larry, *A Colossal Failure of Common Sense: The Incredible Inside Story of the Collapse of Lehman Brothers* (London: Ebury, 2009)

Niederhoffer, Victor, *The Education of a Speculator* (New York: Wiley, 1998)

Pettifor, Ann, *The Production of Money: How to Break the Power of Bankers* (London: Verso, 2017)

Prins, Nomi, *Collusion: How Central Bankers Rigged the World* (New York: PublicAffairs, 2018)

Rothstein, Adam, *The End of Money: The Story of Bitcoin, Cryptocurrencies and the Blockchain Revolution* (London: John Murray, 2017)

Ryan-Collins, Josh, Tony Greenham, Richard Werner, and Andrew Jackson, *Where Does Money Come From? A Guide to the UK Monetary and Banking System* (London: New Economics Foundation, 2017)

Slater, Martin, *The National Debt: A Short History* (London: Hurst Publishers, 2018)

Taleb, Nassim Nicholas, *The Black Swan: The Impact of the Highly Improbable* (London: Penguin, 2008)

Tooze, Adam, *Crashed: How a Decade of Financial Crises Changed the World* (London: Penguin, 2019)

Varoufakis, Yanis, *Talking to My Daughter: A Brief History of Capitalism* (London: Vintage, 2019)

White, Michael, *Isaac Newton: The Last Sorcerer* (London: Fourth Estate, 1997)

Acknowledgements

This book has been a labour of love for over four years and has gone through various iterations during that time before emerging in this form.

My first thanks must go to my late father, Glyn Davies, Emeritus Professor of Economics, whose greatest work, besides creating a wonderful family, was his book *A History of Money*. His love of the subject and fascination with the academic aspects of money were the backdrop to my childhood and helped me enormously in my own life, both academic and practical. That book has been my companion throughout the writing of this one.

My father opened a bank account for me when I was seven years old and paid in my pocket money, inspiring in me a love of saving and a fascination with compound returns that has stayed with me to this day.

Huge thanks are due to St Edmund Hall, University of Oxford, first for giving me a place as an undergraduate to read Politics, Philosophy and Economics – a wonderful triumvirate that allowed me to look at the world of money from three crucial, overlapping and complementary perspectives – and then, several decades later, for inviting me back for a wonderful term as their inaugural writer-in-residence for Michaelmas 2018. Fed, inspired and befriended by them, I continued, deepened and completed an early draft of this work during that time.

I owe Dimitri Tsomocos, Professor of Financial Economics at Saïd Business School and a Fellow in Management at St Edmund Hall, a huge debt for patiently and kindly reading through the manuscript and offering invaluable insights and commentary.

Alexander Chartres, Investment Director at Ruffer LLP, not only gave me two fascinating tours of Ruffer's wonderful collection of financial-themed art, cartoons and objets, but read through several drafts of this book and also gave me invaluable comments and guidance.

I was given a tour of the mysterious virtual world of bitcoin and cryptos by Will Asbury. Thank you for your patience, Will.

My brothers Roy and Kenneth have also very kindly read through the manuscript and made very useful suggestions. We all miss our other brother, the late John Davies, who, like our late father, was an economics professor. He would have made many a piquant and helpful comment and would have had a good laugh at the humour herein.

Some very kind friends have also read through different drafts, which has been a very helpful exercise. Elizabeth Talbot, Carl Fisher and the entire Fisher clan, Anthony Rice and Kevin Regan, thank you all.

I want to thank my wonderful publishers, Atebol, and Owain Saunders-Jones and Rachel Lloyd in particular, for encouraging me through the various iterations of this book until it emerged in this final form. It is so important to work with people you like and respect and who make the process joyful. You guys have done that in spades. Gareth Davies and Heulwen Davies are also a joy to work with, so thank you Team Atebol! The cover designer Tom Burns has done a fantastic job, thank you Tom. And Dr Harri Roberts has been an invaluable copy editor. Thank you Dr Harri!

Nick Bashall, artist extraordinaire and old friend, has brought an added dimension to this book, first with his brilliant cartoons, and second, by being immense fun to work with. This collaboration is the result of a throwaway comment, many years back. My deepest thanks go to him.

I have written hundreds of thousands of words, cut many, and rewritten many more, but all along, through the multiple drafts, some of which he has listened to, some of which he has read aloud to me, has been my husband Rupert – supportive, kind, occasionally bravely and annoyingly critical. He has nurtured me on this money journey, held the domestic fort during my absence as writer-in-residence at St Edmund Hall, Oxford, been a precious sounding board and a tenacious finder of facts. My deepest thanks to him.

Notes

Chapter One: What is money? The biggest confidence trick of all time

1   In the UK, 97 % of our money exists only as squiggles on a computer screen.
2   Tally sticks were essentially one piece of wood or bone broken in two lengthways. One side was retained by the borrower, the other by the lender. The amount in question was notched on each half of the stick. Put together, they matched, an unforgeable record of who owed what to whom. The tally was still used in the twentieth century in rural economies along the Danube river and in Switzerland.
3   One of the Rothschilds, said, possibly apocryphally, in a testament to the power of governments to print money: 'give me the printing press and I'll give you all the guns in the world'.
4   See https://www.britishmuseum.org/collection/object/W_1891-0509-2377

Chapter Two: Where does money come from? The strange magic of new money

1   The remaining 18 per cent of money within the UK economy (data provided by the Bank of England) is held by banks who have accounts with the Bank of England, allowing them to transfer money back and forth. This is called electronic central bank money or reserves.
2   In this context, 'nominal' means the headline rate of interest as opposed to the 'real' rate of interest, which equates to the nominal rate minus the inflation rate, e.g. if the nominal rate of interest is 6 per cent and the rate of inflation is 4 per cent then the 'real' interest rate is 2 per cent. This attempts to capture the real increase in your income, encapsulating what it can actually buy, rather than the apparent rate. You should always examine 'nominal' measures thoroughly to find the 'real' measures they conceal to get a fuller and more useful picture of the value of whatever is being measured.
3   Bank reserve ratios can be used as a tool of monetary policy since they adjust the funds that banks have available to loan. Reserve requirements are also aimed at shielding the banking system from sudden dips in liquidity that

typically occur during financial crises. Less financially robust economies tend to have higher reserve requirements. Brazil has a 20 per cent reserve requirement and Lebanon 30 per cent.

4   This kind of money (which of course looks indistinguishable from state-produced money) is known by academics as 'outside money', as opposed to the 'inside money' which is printed by the state. The creation of new money by banks via fractional reserve lending lies midway along the spectrum between commodity money and fiat money. Again, it is predicated on trust, and, as long as the state produces new money in which we trust, then this 'outside money' also becomes trusted by association.

5   And, much more worryingly, as part of their QE operations, the central banks began to buy up debt issued by companies as well as buying government debt. And they weren't just buying the good stuff, the debt issued by those companies with a triple-A debt rating. In a staggering act of financial malprudence, they have been buying mortgage-backed securities as well. These were the very instruments of destruction that caused the global financial crisis of 2008–09 in the first place. This corporate debt will be much riskier and much more likely to default (go bankrupt) than debt issued by the state and is storing up big problems for the economy come the next financial crisis and/or recession. This practice really is a kind of alchemy, turning base metals into gold.

6   The Bank of England's own research in 2012 showed that quantitative easing made the richest 5 per cent of the population more than £128,000 better off on average.

Chapter Three: What is the future of money? Rebels and revolution

1   These figures are derived from a Morgan Stanley research report.

2   Patrick Jenkins, in the 'Global Economy' section, *FT Magazine* (10 May 2018).

3   According to research by Capgemini and BNP Paribas.

4   See her 'Chair's Blog' at https://www.accesstocash.org.uk/media/1164/chairs-blog-060319-times-red-box-amended-letterhead.pdf. According to Payments UK and the Bank of England, an extra 500,000 people relied on cash between 2016 to 2018.

5   In *The House of the Dead* (1862).

6   https://news.sky.com/story/tsb-on-its-knees-over-online-banking-fiasco-says-boss-11347650

7   A report published by G4S – a global integrated security company – on 17 April 2018, which concludes that worldwide cash use is actually on the rise.

8   According to the Office for National Statistics composite price index, prices in 2018 were 29.98 per cent higher than average prices throughout 2008. In other words, £100 in 2008 is equivalent in purchasing power to about £129.98 in 2018, a difference of £29.98 over ten years.

9   Quoted in *The Times* (30 November 2019).

10 See this excellent resource on mental health and debt: https://images6.moneysavingexpert.com/images/documents/mentalhealthguide_latest.pdf
11 According to a report by McKinsey and Co.
12 Report by Payments Industry Intelligence.
13 That is, part of an oligopoly, a market containing only a small number of producers or sellers where there is only limited competition.
14 See Anne Boden, *The Money Revolution: Easy Ways to Manage Your Finances in a Digital World* (London: Kogan Page, 2019).

Chapter Four: How to multiply money – the eighth wonder of the world

1 This kind of fund buys shares in a range of companies quoted on various exchanges where they can be bought and sold – for example, the FTSE 100, the Financial Times Stock Exchange 100 Index of the hundred biggest companies trading in the UK. By buying into this fund as opposed to buying shares in a single company, you effectively avoid putting your eggs all in one basket and instead diversify your risks. In an ideal world, investing with a good fund manager who can *actively* manage a share portfolio is likely to lead to higher returns. If you are confident that you can find and trust such a manager then this should be the preferred option, as long as the fees they charge are competitive. Tracker funds have dangers of their own – such as the ability to destabilize markets – See note 13 from Chapter Five below.
2 There are a number of bloggers writing about their experience of FIRE and how they have made it work for them. See thehumblepenny.com and theescapeartist.me among many others.
3 See https://inews.co.uk/inews-lifestyle/money/playing-with-fire-financial-method-secret-early-retirement-381343
4 See https://www.bbc.com/worklife/article/20181101-fire-the-movement-to-live-frugally-and-retire-decades-early

Chapter Five: How to invest money – the stock market, property, liquid assets and reckless conservatism

1 The bond market is a huge savage beast of raw power. Back in the 1990s, Democratic political adviser James Carville remarked: 'I used to think that if there was reincarnation, I wanted to come back as the president or the pope or as a .400 baseball hitter. But now I would like to come back as the bond market. You can intimidate everybody.' Leave it to a professional investment manager if you wish to invest in the bond markets (they can do fancy things in the search for value). However, due to the addiction of central banks to quantitative easing (QE), interest rates are at all-time lows, and are even negative in some cases. This means that the medium- to long-term direction of prices in the bond market is DOWN.
2 https://www.moneysavingexpert.com/savings/best-financial-advisers/

3   Data courtesy of the financial services group True Potential.

4   Source: True Potential.

5   One of the pioneers of creating investment vehicles whereby those of modest means could access the stock market was David Hopkinson, who died in October 2019. His company, M&G, created the UK's first unit trust in 1931 and created a 'thrift plan' in 1954 which allowed savers to make regular monthly contributions.

6   According to data from Lipper.

7   Quoted in the *Sunday Times* (15 March 2020).

8   Data from Swanlowpark, a company providing historical data and comparison tools for savers in the UK.

9   According to research by Schroders.

10 A benchmark is a standard against which the performance of an individual equity, fund or investment manager can be measured. For example, a fund investing in large UK companies will use the FTSE 100, the index of larger quoted UK companies, as a benchmark. If the manager is to justify the fees they charge you to invest your money, they should outperform the benchmark, on average, over time.

11 One such, the Ceres coalition (Coalition for Environmentally Responsible Economies), represents over sixty institutional investors from the United States and Europe who manage over $4 trillion in assets and seek to promote investments which are environmentally, socially and economically sound.

12 https://www.moneyadviceservice.org.uk/en/articles/tracker-funds-index-funds-exchange-traded-funds#where-to-get-a-tracker-fund-or-exchange-traded-fund

13 If the price of a particular stock is being driven up (for whatever reason) relative to the rest of the index or benchmark, passive funds will automatically buy more of that stock, driving the price up still more, and so on ad infinitum. By distorting the price mechanism heavily, markets convey less reliable information than in the past and contribute to bubbles.

14 Read more about how to invest in property funds here: https://www.financial-ombudsman.org.uk/businesses/complaints-deal/investments/property-funds

15 Or, indeed, in equities via open-ended funds, as those who invested in Neil Woodford's Equity Income fund discovered to their cost. See https://www.yourmoney.com/investing/woodford-equity-income-fund-a-step-closer-to-being-wound-up/

16 Statistics from Foxtons show that, between 2000 and 2019, the average house price in Hampstead rose from £408,613 to £1,454,610, an average annual increase of 13 per cent.

17 This and following figures are derived from the MoneySavingExpert's Ultimate Mortgage Calculator: https://www.moneysavingexpert.com/mortgages/mortgage-rate-calculator/

18 As of February 2018 (according to World Gold Council figures quoted by the gold dealer BullionStar), the United States held 75 per cent of its reserves in gold, Germany 70 per cent, Italy 67.5 per cent and France 64.9 per cent.

19 The Bundesbank, which maintains most of Germany's gold reserves domestically but also keeps gold in New York and London, states: 'Gold is a type of emergency reserve which can also be used in crisis situations when currencies come under pressure.' It adds: 'In the event of a crisis, the gold could be pledged as collateral or sold at the storage site abroad, without having to be transported. In this way, the Bundesbank could raise liquidity in a foreign reserve currency.' The Bank of England's 'Handbook on Foreign Exchange Reserves Management' cites these traditional reasons for holding gold:

- the 'war chest' argument – gold is seen as the ultimate asset to hold in an emergency and in the past has often appreciated in value in times of financial instability or uncertainty
- the ultimate store of value, inflation hedge and medium of exchanges – gold has traditionally kept its value against inflation and has always been accepted as a medium of exchange between countries
- no default risk – gold is 'nobody's liability' and so cannot be frozen, repudiated or defaulted on
- gold's historical role in the international monetary system as the ultimate backing for domestic paper money

For further information, see https://www.bullionstar.com/blogs/ronan-manly/worlds-central-banks-hold-gold-words/

20 The gold price in June 2007 was £322 per ounce, rising to £1,155 per ounce by September 2011.

21 A gold ETF, or exchange-traded fund, owns one principal asset, gold, accessed by buying gold derivative contracts backed by gold. Exchange-traded funds act like individual stocks, being bought and sold on an exchange in the same way.

22 This article offers more detailed information on how to invest in gold: https://www.thisismoney.co.uk/money/investing/article-1666644/How-invest-gold-including-coins-funds-ETCs-bullion.html#socialLinks

23 Quoted in the *Daily Telegraph* (2 November 2019).

24 According to Stanley Gibbons's GB250 Index.

25 *The Times* (9 November 2019).

26 Check out potential investment managers on the Financial Services Register (https://register.fca.org.uk/) to see if they are authorized or have been connected with any scams.

Chapter Six: How to lose money – 'Brown's Bottom', burning money and vampire notes

1 Hyperinflation is a sustained increase in prices, generally agreed by economists to exceed 50 per cent per month. At a monthly rate of 50 per cent, something that cost £1 on 1 January would cost £130 by 1 January of the following year.

2   The United States has suffered two interesting periods of hyperinflation, the first during the American Revolutionary War (1775–83) and the second during the American Civil War (1861–65). For an extended discussion, see Glyn Davies, *A History of Money* (4th edn, Cardiff: University of Wales Press, 2016).

3   Costantino Bresciani-Turroni, *The Economics of Inflation: A Study of Currency Depreciation in Post-War Germany*, tr. Millicent E. Sayers (3rd impr., New York: Augustus M. Kelley, 1968), p. 440.

4   Source: Bullionmark.

5   Quotation from https://www.spiegel.de/international/germany/millions-billions-trillions-germany-in-the-era-of-hyperinflation-a-641758.html (accessed 19 July 2020).

6   Quoted ibid.

7   Movements in the price of gold during the Weimar hyperinflation confirmed its role as what's known as an inflation 'hedge', i.e. a means of protection and counterbalance.

Chapter Seven: How to steal money – buying time, multiple shades of grey, naughty money and castration

1   Hedge funds are pools of money provided by 'sophisticated' investors deemed able to assess the risks of investing in such pools. They are less regulated than mutual funds and other investment vehicles available to the general public. They can use a wide range of financial tools to attempt to make money in both rising and falling markets, on occasion controversially by 'shorting' financial assets, i.e. selling assets that they don't actually own in the belief that they can buy them later at a lower price (thereby exploiting the 'buy low, sell high' mantra, albeit in reverse). They are owned and run by financial professionals often deemed to be (particularly by themselves) the most aggressive and successful of their generation.

2   Quotation from https://www.bankofengland.co.uk/banknotes/counterfeit-banknotes (accessed 21 July 2020).

Chapter Eight: Money and children – how to raise financially literate children and how to invest for them. Angels, Demons and gender

1   According to a 2019 article by the Money Charity, only 38 per cent of young people between 7 and 17 years of age say they learned about how to manage money at school.

2   Quote adapted from CHILDWISE press release: http://www.childwise.co.uk/uploads/3/1/6/5/31656353/childwise_press_release_-_money_and_finance_2017.pdf (accessed 22 July 2020).

3   Dr David Whitebread and Dr Sue Bingham, 'Habit Formation and Learning in Young Children' (May 2013). The study was commissioned by the Money Advice Service.

4   The Money Advice Service revealed in a study in 2018 that a pilot course to help parents teach their children about money also improved parents' finances. Twelve months after taking the course, there was a 15 percentage point decrease in the number of overindebted parents.

5   Tracker funds are made up of a weighted representation of the constituent companies of, in this particular case, what is known as the FTSE 100 – the Financial Times index of shares in the 100 leading companies quoted on the London Stock Exchange.

6   Calculations based on £5 a week, equating to £21.67 per month. Compounding frequency is monthly.

7   APR stands for annual percentage rate. It differs from the interest rate because as well as interest costs it incorporates fees related to a loan.

8   According to the Money Charity in 2019.

9   There is an excellent 2018 article on skin gambling by ParentZone.

10   Sally Monaghan, Jeffrey Derevensky and Alyssa Sklar, 'Impact of gambling advertisements and marketing on children and adolescents: policy recommendations to minimise harm', *Journal of Gambling Issues*, 22 (2008), 252–74. An electronic version of this article can be downloaded here: http://jgi.camh.net/index.php/jgi/article/view/3802/3807 (accessed 22 July 2020).

11   The NHS surveyed more than 8,000 adults and 2,000 children, reporting results in 2019.

12   The elevated risk remained even when corrected for other contributing factors that might be linked to suicidal thoughts, such as depression, substance abuse and financial problems. Stripping out such factors, the researchers found that problem gamblers were still three times more likely to consider or attempt suicide.

13   Quoted in *The Times* (19 April 2020).

Chapter Nine: Money, psychology and you – how to identify and monetise your psychology

1   Elaine M. Liu and Sharon Xuejing Zuo, 'Measuring the impact of interaction between children of a matrilineal and a patriarchal culture on gender differences in risk aversion' (2019). Article available at: https://www.pnas.org/content/116/14/6713 (accessed 24 July 2020).

2   Quote adapted from an article in *Newsweek* (18 March 2019) available at https://www.newsweek.com/women-risk-adverse-society-teaches-study-1364860 (accessed 24 July 2020).

3   There are various versions of this quote floating around the internet.

4   See Sherree DeCovny, 'The Financial Psychopath Next Door', *CFA Institute Magazine*, 23/2 (March–April 2012), where it is claimed that 10 per cent (at least) of those working in the financial services industry are psychopaths. Available at: https://www.cfainstitute.org/en/research/cfa-magazine/2012/the-financial-psychopath-next-door (accessed 24 July 2020).

5   The title of a 2018 book by Taleb.

6   Charline Uhr, Steffen Meyer and Andreas Hackethal, 'Smoking Hot Portfolios? Overtrading from Self-Control Failure' (September 2019). SAFE Working Paper No. 245. Available at: https://www.ssrn.com/abstract=3347625 (accessed on 24 July 2020). Separating out smokers who manage their own investments changes the picture. These tobacco-fuelled DIY investors held less diversified portfolios and underperformed both with regard to non-smokers and tobacco users who had hired finance professionals, according to the paper.

7   Study published in June 2018.

8   Published in August 2017.

9   Published in *Quarterly Journal of Economics*, 116/1 (February 2001), 261–92.

10   Quoted in the *Financial Times* (29 April 2019).

11   A study by Netwealth, an online adviser, published in March 2019 to coincide with International Woman's Day, revealed that ISAs held by women aged 45–54 are worth an average of 19 per cent less than those of men.

Chapter Ten: Money, psychology and the market – booms, busts, animal spirits, greater fools and crises; how not to get trampled by the herd and how to bolster your financial resilience

1   Professor Knight was one of the seminal thinkers in the realm of uncertainty in economics, the formulator of what's become known in academe as 'Knightean uncertainty'. Quote taken from his book *Risk, Uncertainty and Profit* (1921).

2   By the way, we need the Tiggers in our world. They are the entrepreneurs, the inventors, the pioneers: those who have a higher than average tolerance of risk, uncertainty and ambiguity and are excited and challenged by it. We just need to keep an eye on them. In *Financial Regulation and Stability* (2019), economists Charles Goodhart and Dimitrios P. Tsomocos outline a method of measuring the effects of the Tiggers and reining them in before they get carried away.

3   The word *Torschlusspanik* (literally 'gate-shut panic' – from when city gates used to be shut at nightfall leaving latecomers exposed to danger outside) is one of those wonderful German compound nouns (like *Weltanschauung* and *schadenfreude*) and describes the fear that time is running out in which to act.

4   According to historian Mike Dash in his fascinating book *Tulipomania: the story of the world's most coveted flower and the extraordinary passions it aroused* (W&N, 2010).

5   Algorithms that attempt to capture the emotion of the markets do exist. One such, the VIX, is known as the Fear Index.

6   The quote is commonly attributed to Ford but it may well be a pithy summary of his beliefs rather than a direct quotation.

7   The Bank of England, as of 2018, estimated that the sub-prime crisis has cost

the world's financial institutions $2.8 trillion. Paper losses from UK banks on mortgage-backed securities and corporate bonds were valued at £122.6 billion. In cash terms, the UK government has so far spent £133 billion according to the National Audit Office.

8   Data courtesy of Statista.

9   Moral hazard exists in situations where participants have an incentive to do something which is potentially or actively damaging to others.

10 The index published by the National Association of Realtors showed that median house prices dropped by 18 per cent in six months in late 2008. The S&P Case–Shiller Index showed a 25 per cent drop over twenty-seven months, the largest drop in almost ninety years.

11 Shorting is basically selling something you don't have at a high price then buying it when the price has fallen so you can deliver the asset to the original buyer and pocket the difference.

12 I have to thank Nassim Nicholas Taleb for introducing the world to the concept of black swans. See his book *The Black Swan: The Impact of the Highly Improbable* (London: Penguin, 2008).

13 Widely attributed to Shaw though likely a paraphrase from a passage in his play *Back to Methuselah* (1921).

14 A stock market index that measures the stock performance of 500 large companies listed on stock exchanges in the United States.

Money miscellany

1   This and subsequent quotations can be found on Crawford's website, crawfordperspectives.com (accessed 27 July 2020).

2   In *Financial Regulation and Stability*, economists Charles Goodhart and Dimitrios P. Tsomocos outline a method of measuring that fire and offer a means of dampening it before it turns into an inferno.

3   Information from the House of Commons Library.

Also by Linda Davies

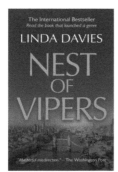  

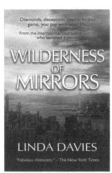 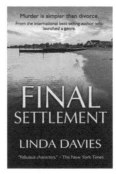 

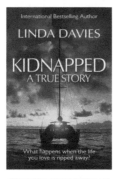  

Linda Davies

Linda graduated in Politics, Philosophy and Economics from Oxford University and then put theory into practice as an investment banker in New York, London and Eastern Europe. After eight years, she escaped to write what went on to become the international bestselling financial thriller that launched a new genre, *Nest of Vipers*.

Linda has written thirteen books of fiction, non-fiction and children's books. Linda also writes for *The Times*, *Sunday Times*, *Daily Telegraph*, *Independent*, *The Guardian* and *The Daily Express* newspapers in the UK. In 2018, she was selected to become the inaugural Writer in Residence at St Edmund Hall, University of Oxford. She retains an active interest in the financial world as a company director and consultant.

You can get in touch or follow Linda here:

lindadavies.com

@LindaDaviesAuth

@lindawriter1

Nick Bashall

Nick is one of the UK's leading portrait artists having painted everyone from HRH Princess Anne to General Sir Michael Jackson to Linda Davies. This is his first book and in a series of hilarious and brilliantly-observed cartoons, Nick brings the money world to life in a way you've never seen it before.

Born in England and raised in Zimbabwe, Nick returned to the UK to study law at Cambridge, where he was also a heavyweight boxer. Having worked in London, Pakistan and Dubai he saved enough money to study painting full-time in Majorca, before becoming a full-time artist in London in 1997. Nick performs as a painter alongside DJs at major festivals such as Glastonbury and also at private events, where audiences enjoy his canvases coming to life.

You can get in touch or follow Nick here:

↖ nickbashall.com

⊙ nickbashall.artist